Walking in the Light

---◆◆---

A daily guidebook for enhancing peace, love, and connection

Nancy Rynes

Project editor: Amy Collette Casey

All rights reserved. No part of this book may be reproduced by any means; nor may it be stored in a retrieval system, transmitted, or otherwise copied for public or private use — other than "fair use" as short quotations in articles or reviews — without prior written permission of the author.

DISCLAIMER: The author of this book does not dispense any medical or psychological advice, or prescribe the use of any technique as a form of treatment for physical, medical, emotional, or mental health problems without the advice of a physician or other trained professional, either directly or indirectly. The intent of the author is only to offer information from her own experience, and of a general nature to help you in your quest for spiritual understanding and well-being. In the event you use any of the information in this book for yourself, which is your right, the author assumes no responsibility for your actions.

If you are experiencing physical, medical, emotional, or spiritual issues, the author advises you to seek the advice of an appropriate professional (medical doctor, psychotherapist, counselor, etc.).

Library of Congress Cataloging-in-Publication Data

Rynes, Nancy
Walking in the Light — A daily guidebook for enhancing peace, love, and connection

ISBN: 978-0-692-89708-9

Author's Proof Edition edition, March 2021 (limited to 100 copies)

Printed in the United States of America

Copyright © 2021 Nancy Rynes

Dedication

To everyone who needs peace and comfort right now, this book is for you.

Acknowledgements

Thank you to all of my readers and followers who have been asking for a book like this.

Thank you to my friend and editor, Amy Collette. Your graceful attention to this book helped it grow and blossom.

To my first reviewers, fellow authors, and Mastermind Members: Amy Collette, Christine Moriarty, Lynn Robinson, and Jeff Janssen. Your input vastly improved the content and flow of this book, and your friendship and support over the last few years has helped me more than you will ever know.

To Ken Elliott and Marianne Pestana. Your support over the last few years has been invaluable.

A big thanks also to Judy Goodman, a valued spiritual mentor whose input helped make this book deeper and more meaningful.

Thank you, John Crandall, for your heartfelt conversations, support, and friendship.

Deep gratitude goes to my family and especially my sister, Mary Jo Rynes, for standing by me though a very challenging 2020!

To my dear friend, Marilyn Ryan. Thank you for you friendship, conversations, strength, and support for more decades than I care to admit!

And I would like to give a special nod of appreciation to Kathy Duxbury whose belief in, and support of, this book made its publication possible. Thank you.

Contents

Welcome	6
Week 1: Love	16
Week 2: Love Yourself	34
Week 3: Love the Earth	52
Week 4: Creativity	70
Week 5: Connections	88
Week 6: Releasing and Allowing	106
Week 7: Building Community	124
Week 8: Intuition	142
Week 9: Choice	160
Week 10: Gratitude	178
Week 11: Expanding Your Perspective	196
Week 12: Uniquely You	216
Three Month Review	233
Next Steps	238
Celebrate Your Wins	240
Additional Practices	246
Additional Resources	254
About Nancy	256

1 Welcome

What if I told you that you have all of the ingredients for a more peaceful, loving, and connected life within you right now? Would you believe me?

Trust me when I say that you absolutely do.

No matter where you are on your spiritual journey, no matter your religious affiliation, personal philosophy, or challenges you face, you have the capacity to live a more present, centered, peaceful, connected, and loving life. By taking a little time each day to devote to simple but meaningful readings and exercises, you absolutely *can* create the life you desire.

I won't lie to you. Achieving this takes a little bit of dedicated time and attention each day, but it doesn't have to consume every waking moment either. In fact, it can be a relatively simple process that eventually just becomes a normal part of your life.

I have designed this book so that the concepts come to you in bite-sized chunks, divided up day-by-day so you can take small steps toward living the more peace-filled and loving life you deserve. It is not intended to replace any organized religion or belief system but instead act as an adjunct, giving you additional concepts to consider and practices to try.

Through this book, I share with you the basic methods I used to craft a more peaceful, centered life for myself. How did I do this? I formed a daily habit of simple readings and exercises which helped me stay more aware and peaceful in the present moment, and trust Spirit[1] and the flow of life much more than I ever had previously. While it might sound almost *too* simple, I want you to know that this gradual process of learning and growth had its genesis in two physically painful, yet profound and life-altering near-death experiences (NDEs)[2]. During these experiences, I came to understand that a Higher Power *does* exist, that It is all-encompassing love, and that there is much more to this grand, spiritual, and conscious universe than I had ever imagined. But it took time, patience, research, and practice in order to better use my NDE to craft the life I have today.

The good news for you is that I have used myself as a test subject over the last several years, figuring out what works, what does not, and what is too complicated to fit into a typical life. With that knowledge I have distilled my approach down to relatively simple concepts and practices that can help you achieve a more grounded, present, and peaceful life in a relatively short amount of time. Over the next several weeks, you will learn what took me over five years of research, study, and practice to develop and incorporate into my own life.

Contrary to what many believe, a spiritual experience such as an NDE doesn't automatically transform someone into a guru or a saint. Experiences such as these are

---

[1] In this book, I typically use the term "Spirit" to refer to our Higher Power. Sometimes I will use "the Divine." Both refer to that same loving, all-encompassing consciousness that many refer to as God, Creator, etc. Substitute in whatever term is most comfortable and meaningful for you.

[2] Detailed in my book *Awakenings from the Light*.

simply invitations, gateways, and perhaps even glimpses into a grander view of reality. They prompt us to open our hearts and minds to the limitless love of Spirit, and many times ask us to change our lives into ones that bring peace and love to this planet. But experiencers still have work to do once the event itself ends. We must learn how to take this new knowledge and expanded awareness into our hearts, all while using it to help ourselves live better lives.

Integrating this profound love, peace, and expanded awareness into our ordinary lives isn't always straightforward, whether we have had a profound experience or not. Experiencers are usually not given a blueprint of how to make this happen, especially if, like me, we are starting from square zero with relatively little education in religious or spiritual concepts. So after I physically recovered from my accident and felt ready to dive in to the spiritual part of my journey, I decided to revisit what I learned during my first NDE.

That NDE taught me above all that the Divine is *LOVE*, all-encompassing and all-inclusive. If the only thing we do in life is learn to really *be* love and share that love with everyone else, that is enough. I also learned that the way we treat ourselves and others is vitally important to expanding our awareness and sense of inner peace. Our actions and choices matter in helping improve our lives, and can contribute to strengthening Divine love on this planet. And I learned that we are all connected to each other, this planet, and the universe whether we want to admit it or not. Whatever we do to, and for, others comes back to us as individuals.

Driven by the desire to recreate the peace and love I experienced in heaven here in my life on Earth, I began taking small, daily steps to change my life. I started by reading and writing about Spirit and spiritual topics, and began a contemplative practice of prayer and mindfulness. I set intentions each morning, then reviewed my day before I went to sleep for the night. Deep gratitude became a daily practice, as did strengthening my connections with loved ones. Over time, my awareness shifted so that I felt more peace-filled, joyous, and loving every day.

The methods that I created for myself, that helped me achieve so much peace and joy, form the core of this book.

A Sacred Journey

A doorway to another world opened for me during my first NDE in 2014. Spirit brought me across the threshold of death to glimpse a reality I had denied for too long. I did not know at the time that my initial, brief view into the spiritual world, while tantalizing and mesmerizing, was simply the first step in what has since turned into a passion and lifelong journey. [3]

The truth is that spiritual experiences come in many guises, each one different, but most, if not all, offering something that has the potential to affect powerful change in the experiencer. They offer the opportunity to dive deeply into the profound nature of spirituality, the outer limits of consciousness, and what it means to be alive. They invite us to contemplate the reality of different planes of existence, the depth and beauty of our own souls, our connections to history, and the illusions of time and physicality. Spiritual experiences ask us to deepen our connections to each other, and mature into

---

[3] My near-death experience (NDE) and the teachings I gained from it are detailed in my book *Awakenings from the Light*.

our power as children of that Divine, expansive, spiritual consciousness.

In the end, if we are diligent and perhaps a little bit lucky, we might even see a few tantalizing glimpses of the true workings of the universe along the way.

Spiritual experiences can be invitations to start a journey toward a greater level of awareness, but the journey to awakening and awareness more often begins *without* a profound experience. The internal desire for a life of more meaning and authenticity is an invitation all its own. That desire can well up from deep within our beings, asking us to seek out a life that is more present, meaningful, joy-filled, free, aware, and peaceful.

These different types of invitations are but the first steps on each person's sacred, spiritual journey.

No one type of experience and no one type of calling is better than the others on the path toward a more loving and peace-filled life. All are equally valid, be they visions, shared death experiences, near-death experiences (like mine), kundalini experiences, gradual awakenings, or the quiet desire of the heart for a life of deeper meaning and connection. All give the invitee, the initiate, an opportunity to deepen his or her understanding and connection to ideas and realities far greater than what they may have learned as children, and far more than modern science cares to admit.

When we truly accept that invitation and step through the doorway, we have been initiated onto the path of a seeker and will never be the same. Peace, freedom, Divine love, and expansive consciousness awaits, along with our intimate connection to all in the spiritual realms.

While this journey will be unique to each traveler, we all have one thing in common: we must embrace some form of incremental, consistent process of learning, growth, exploration, fun, and curiosity in order to fully reap the benefits the path has in store. There is one problem, though. Many of us in the modern world don't even understand what spiritual practice is, let alone how to put one together and what the benefits might be. In this book, I have done the bulk of this work for you by introducing you to my own methods and practices as a starting point.

After my first NDE, I struggled for months with trying to make sense out of what happened, and then many more months beyond that to figure out how to go forward with what I learned. Finally, about eighteen months after my experience, I had one of those aha moments when I realized that:

1. My NDE was simply an invitation to begin a journey. It was not a spiritual destination in and of itself.
2. I had an amazing opportunity in front of me to make my life more peaceful and meaningful by following a spiritual path.
3. The lessons I learned during my NDE were everything I needed to start on the path to achieving a peaceful more meaningful life.
4. A journey toward personal, spiritual improvement would need to be a consistent yet simple practice in order to work for me.

I began to build peace and love into my life slowly, one exercise at a time. I did not have the time or patience to meditate or pray for hours on end each day, or go on a two-year spiritual retreat. Don't get me wrong; I knew these things were appropriate and helpful for some people, they just did not fit into my life. I wanted to be challenged to improve, but I also needed a spiritual path that allowed me to spend time with family and friends, maintain a job, and have fun.

I asked myself what I desired in my life. My list included:

- More peace
- More presence, or *present moment awareness*
- More joy
- Deeper connections to people around me, and to Spirit
- More love
- Enhanced creativity

I also wanted to be free of anxiety, fear, and regret while at the same time be more fully focused on, and present in, the *now* moment. With that in mind, I started incorporating short exercises into my day that I hoped, in time, would help me achieve these, and more.

At a high level, what helped me the most were:

- Starting off my day with a spiritual reading, prayers, and intentions
- Finishing up my day with reflection and gratitude
- Learning ways to quiet my mind without hours of daily meditation
- Being grateful throughout the day
- Helping others
- Taking care of my body
- Being curious and always looking for the lesson
- Practicing love, compassion, and kindness with my words and actions
- Making time for fun and play

Life Review

One of the most powerful aspects of near-death experiences (NDEs) is what we call the life review. This is a point after death where the soul may be presented with events from his or her life in order to review actions, intentions, and lessons learned. The soul may be shown a time when he caused harm to another, or helped someone through a challenging situation. The life review is not a tool for punishment but is instead a pathway for learning and growth. As a result of a life review, it is often the case where the soul gains greater compassion, empathy, and spiritual insight, and achieves a deeper understanding of how to go forward, helping themselves and others in more meaningful ways.

My own life review was a powerful catalyst for personal growth during my NDE, so I incorporated its concepts into my days. At the end of each day, I journaled (briefly) about what went well, what did not go so well, what I could learn from these things, and how to approach tomorrow. This end-of-day reflection forms the core of the evening exercises in this book. If it is too much for you to answer all of the questions, choose one or two and answer them consistently each day. Keeping your answers brief but meaningful will help you more than writing long journal entries each night.

Crafting Your Own Practice

My goal with this book is to give you a daily model or script that will help you begin to see the benefits of a regular, spiritual habit for yourself. Ultimately, my hope is that you use this model as a starting point to craft your own practice, one that most closely fits your life.

While this book contains some of the core techniques that worked for me, I understand that there are many ways to achieve greater spiritual awareness and peace. Your religious or spiritual organization may have other methods that work just as well for you, or even better. If you want to try new methods, my suggestion is to experiment with one at a time, giving each at least three weeks of regular attention before deciding if it will be helpful for you.

I now look on my time here on this planet as a sacred journey, a spiritual practice in its own right. Simply being here on Earth, living consciously from a place of love, awareness, and centered presence, is my main spiritual practice now.

Please join me on this journey to the sacred.

> Spirit, today I walk in your love and light.
> All I do and say is from Your love and light.
> Your love and light enfolds me,
> Embraces me,
> And keeps me safely on my best path.
>
> Spirit, thank you for being with me on my journey.[4]

---

[4] This is my basic morning prayer, and was the inspiration for this book's title.

Key to Icons Used in this Book:

 This figure indicates a physical activity.

 The lotus blossom means that this is a contemplative, meditative, or prayer-based practice.

 The heart indicates a practice or message that is focused on love.

 The light bulb icon means that this is an idea or something for you to think about.

 A pencil icon indicates a journaling exercise. These are usually optional but highly recommended. Have a separate journal on hand, or use a file on your computer or mobile device to complete these exercises.

 The gift or giving icon means that this is a practice primarily focused on giving to others.

 A book indicates optional, recommended reading.

Abbreviations used in this book:

AFTL: *Awakenings from the Light* by Nancy Rynes
MFH: *Messages from Heaven* by Nancy Rynes

Before You Begin

What do I want more of in the next three months?

How am I feeling overall right now? (Physical, Emotional, etc.)

What inspires or energizes me?

People I love:

Things I enjoy doing:

I want to learn:

Challenges I am facing:

Additional thoughts:

Peace in the world
starts with
peace in
our
hearts.

Week One: Love

Welcome, and thank you for allowing me to join you for a short time during your sacred, spiritual adventure called life. I am so glad that I can share with you some of the tools and practices that have helped me and my students create more peace-filled, fun, conscious, connected, and inspired lives.

In this first week, you will begin to explore ways to enhance love in your life, to strengthen your connection to Divine love, and forge deeper bonds to those closest to you.

What I refer to as *Divine love* forms the foundation or structure of what we experience as everyday physical reality. It is the underlying, positive, creative, and supportive energy or "field" that ties us all together. Divine love binds us to every other being on this planet, to the planet itself, and ultimately to the entire universe. During my two near-death experiences (NDEs), I felt Divine love as a tangible energy field although it was simultaneously much more than that. We think of energy as the mysterious *thing* that powers a light bulb or a computer, but Divine love is, at its core, the multidimensional structure of the universe. Other authors have called this the Divine Field, the Divine Matrix, or sometimes just "Universe." It is the sacred, loving, conscious, connected energy that forms the framework of all that is.

I experience a vast, loving, intelligent consciousness behind all that we perceive of as reality. We may call this consciousness by any of a number of names depending on our backgrounds and belief systems. In this book, I will refer to this intelligence by the non-denominational terms, "Spirit" and "Divine."

We are an integral part Divine love. Even if we think that we are separate, which is what our human, ego-selves would have us believe, we are absolutely immersed in the Divine field with every breath, thought, and action. That foundational energy of love flows around us and through us, supporting us even when we don't perceive it with our physical senses.

The subject of Divine love is as vast as the universe itself. But this week my goal will be to teach you how to begin to recognize it in your daily life, connect with it more deeply on a conscious level, and allow it to support you through easy practices that you can try for yourself.

Let's get started, shall we?

Extra Credit: Are you a creative person? If so, as you progress through this book I invite you to use your creativity to express any feelings or insights that may come up. Grab your paints, brushes, pencils, clay, dance shoes, or musical instruments and without too much analytical thought, use your intuition and heart to give form to any insights or energies inspired by this book. Feel free to share them with me on social media:
#WITL #SpiritPainting #Inspiration #nancyrynes

(Day 1) Begin Your Day: 4/8/24

"[As my NDE began] I sensed and somehow physically *felt* an incredibly profound feeling of peace, rightness, goodness, and love flowing through my body. I cried, literally wept, at how beautiful it all was and thought to myself that it was definitely an OK place to be during my surgery; much better than that gray nothingness I expected. I didn't know where I stood or how I came here, but I felt at home, right, and at peace.

"The Beauty I saw and felt in those first moments really does deserve a capital 'B.' It wasn't just pleasing to the eye, there was something deeper to it, more harmonious, more blessed, and more powerful. Everything felt tied together by an enormous amount of love and peace. Somehow I knew that the beauty of the landscape around me was the product of unconditional love on a cosmic scale.

"While this beauty took my breath away, the sense of overwhelming peace and love completely ensnared me and made me want to stay here forever. I continued to feel a deep sense of unconditional love flow through all things around me: the air, the ground below my feet, the trees, the clouds, and me. I didn't know how it was possible to feel love as if it were a physical presence, but I did. My being vibrated with love to its core. Every molecule of me seemed bathed in love. I couldn't block it out, nor would I have wanted to. I continued to feel the energy of love flow around me like a gentle current, washing through me, and eventually capturing me by the heart. I felt supported by some kind of loving presence so powerful, yet so gentle, that I cried again. I had never experienced such unconditional love and acceptance in all of my years on this Earth." (AFTL, Chapter 6)

Today's Prayer: *Divine Spirit, allow me to see the love, compassion, and kindness in the world around me today.*

One thing I am grateful for this morning:

Practice for the week: Love walks. See page 254 for more information. Go on love walks at least three times this week.

Extra Credit: Celebrate your wins. Beginning today, take note of all of the good things that happen in your life. Did you accomplish a goal? Get a compliment from a coworker? Receive a new job or a raise? Marry? Adopt a baby? Make note of any and all of the good things that happen to you in the "Celebrate Your Wins" section near the back of this book (page 240). On days when you feel a little down, read through this list of good things to get a pick-me-up and reset your perspective.

End Your Day

What I am grateful for today:

> Gratitude helps you reset your perspective to the good things that you *do* have, right now.

What didn't go so well today?

What did I learn from that?

Good stuff that happened:

How can I make tomorrow better?

(Day 2) Begin Your Day: _____5/3/24_____

"Each person is a part of Spirit. Each is an expression of Divine love — not just those people we count as family or friends, but everyone. When we look into the eyes of another, we are also looking directly at Spirit. Each person is an expression of divinity, a window to the Creator, the Divine Universe, no matter the color of his skin, her religious affiliation, politics, or financial status. How could we not love each person we see, and thus love Spirit more fully through them?" (AFTL, Chapter 6)

Today's Prayer: Divine Spirit, thank you for helping me see the spark of divinity inside those I love.

One thing I am grateful for this morning:

The little message now to his birthday today

Today I Intend to:

Be respectful of myself and take responsibility for my actions. See the Divine in the eyes of those I see.

Be kind and loving to yourself today. You are taking a huge step toward cultivating more peace, awareness, and love in your life. Spend time with someone you love, or participate in an activity you enjoy. Make sure you always take a little time for yourself each day so that you can be there for others when they need you.

Extra Credit: Go back to the "Before You Begin" section on page 12 and think about ways to turn any of these into your daily intentions (above). For example, a desire to finish a college degree might start with an intention of contacting admissions departments.

End Your Day

What I am grateful for today:

What didn't go so well today?

> Thinking about the things that didn't go so well, and then considering what we can learn from them, helps us grow and make more effective decisions in the future.

What did I learn from that?

Good stuff that happened:

How can I make tomorrow better?

Stay in adult mode & take responsibility for helping myself to enjoy life better

(Day 3) Begin Your Day: _____6/8/24_____

Expanding their capacity to love is a common goal for the souls who come here to Earth. Even if a soul has many other things it needs to learn or accomplish during a lifetime, I can pretty much guarantee that learning to expand its capacity to love, especially in challenging situations, is one of them.

During my first NDE, I learned that love isn't just something we feel, it is also an action we take and ultimately how we show up in our lives every day. Being loving is not limited to simple acts of kindness, hugging your kids, or helping those less fortunate. Those are all wonderful and worthwhile, but *being love* is much more than this and can challenge us to our cores. It means consciously extending compassion and kindness to everyone, including yourself, whether you feel an affinity for that other person or not. It means extending the gifts of listening and understanding to others, being truthful and honest in a heartfelt way, and yes, treating all others in the way that you would treat the person who is most dear to you.

Lucky for us perfection isn't required. What is? Truly doing our best, and that takes awareness, courage, grace, and humility.

Today's Prayer: *Spirit, everything I do and say today is from love and light.*

One thing I am grateful for this morning:
I had a better nights sleep - ready for the day in Lincoln.

Today I Intend to:
Enjoy the day.

Challenge for today: Be genuinely kind to someone who doesn't expect it. Buy lunch for a coworker, leave an encouraging note for your kids or spouse, or hold the door open for a stranger. Random acts of kindness help both you and the recipient feel good, and they strengthen the energy of love around you. For more ideas, search for "random acts of kindness" on the internet.

End Your Day

What I am grateful for today:

Lovely day in Lincoln - Sunny day
Good haircut from Becky.

What didn't go so well today?

My being frustrated with Dave for getting us to Lincoln just in time. Behaved immaturely & stressed Dave out. Saying too much to Becky just to chat - it was unnecessary.

What did I learn from that?

How much I still need to improve on my patience & immaturity. How much I must refrain from talking about others to fill in conversation.

Good stuff that happened:

Lovely walk in Lincoln
Great singing from guy who sounded a bit like Tracey Chapman

> Remember to note these good things in the "Celebrate Your Wins" section on page 240.

How can I make tomorrow better?

Behave more maturely.
Don't get unecessarily frustrated. Keep my council on others.
Lord please forgive my behaviour today.

(Day 4) Begin Your Day: _____7/8/24_____

About four years after my first NDE, I traveled to Chicago to visit friends and simply revisit the city nearest and dearest to my heart. Unfortunately, I came back from my trip with an unusual respiratory virus. Within hours of developing my first symptoms, my health fell apart. I found it difficult to breathe and in fact, had stopped breathing on two different occasions. Then my blood pressure dropped to alarmingly low levels and I collapsed three separate times. My next trip was to the emergency room where I collapsed again, then felt my body begin to shut down; a peaceful yet bizarre process that seemed familiar. My vision blurred and went dark, I could no longer hear sound, and my soul-consciousness left my body and drifted up toward the ceiling where it hovered a few feet above the hospital bed. Other bodily systems began shutting down as well, to the point where all that remained of *me* was my soul simply observing my dying body with detached compassion and love.

That's when I felt heavenly bliss, peace, and love once again. I calmly reflected on what was happening and realized this was how most souls exit physical life — peacefully and with deep love and support. Once again I felt cradled in the arms of Spirit as my soul's consciousness hovered in the hospital room, ready to move on.

Then I heard and felt that booming, Divine voice again, speaking directly to my heart. It asked, "Your choice. Stay or go, which will it be?"

I remembered that voice from four years earlier, how it echoed though me when Spirit welcomed me home the first time. It reverberated through my soul this time too, but with a seemingly simple question: stay or go?

I was being given a choice. Without hesitation my heart replied that I wanted to stay to help my daughter create a happy, healthy adult life for herself. And I vaguely remembered a big project that I wanted to finish before I finally ended my time here.

It was done, the decision made. As my body's systems began to engage once again, I felt my soul reunite with my physical self. I knew I had made the right choice for me.

Today's Prayer: *Spirit, thank you for helping me see how amazing my life is.*

One thing I am grateful for this morning:

many things this morning, beautiful day, feel fine

Today I Intend to:

Be the best person I can be for myself and others.

Optional journaling exercise: Get a outside perspective on yourself. Describe your strengths, gifts, talents, and positive personality traits from the vantage point of a friend or loved one. Stay in the positive. Talk yourself up! If you are having trouble with this, actually ask a trusted friend or loved one to help you. What positive qualities do they see in you? Jot them down in your journal.

End Your Day

What I am grateful for today:

What didn't go so well today?

What did I learn from that?

Good stuff that happened:

How can I make tomorrow better?

NB

Spending a little time each day thinking about how you can make things better helps you become more aware of the importance of your intentions and actions.

(Day 5) Begin Your Day: _____8/8/24_____

"During my NDE, my guides said, 'We know that it is easy for you to show love to others when a disaster strikes. So many of you [on Earth] rise up to help during times of crisis: a flood, an earthquake, a severe fire. While we salute you for helping others in these times, for showing love during a crisis, the world needs your love all of the time, not just during a disaster. Helping others on a normal day is just as powerful and necessary an act of love as helping out disaster victims every few years. Do not wait for a disaster to strike to show your love and caring to others. After all, Spirit does not wait for tough times to show love and caring to you. Spiritual love surrounds you all of the time, every day, every night, in good times, and in bad. Try to emulate this pattern in yourself, with those around you. Give love, BE love as much as you can. Your world will be a better place for your efforts.'" (AFTL, Chapter 6)

Today's Prayer: *Spirit, thank you for enfolding me in your love and light, today and every day.*

One thing I am grateful for this morning:

Today I Intend to:

☀ **What activities do you enjoy?** Make a point of doing something that you enjoy today, even if it's only for 10 minutes.

End Your Day

What I am grateful for today:

What didn't go so well today?

What did I learn from that?

Good stuff that happened:

How can I make tomorrow better?

(Day 6) Begin Your Day: _____

Sometimes coming to a place of empathy and compassion can help us forge stronger bonds with the people around us.

Several years ago when I was still working in an office setting, my job consisted of creating training materials for scientists and engineers. The position challenged me, but I had fun working with our company's energetic, brilliant professionals. But there was one coworker (Jane) who I wasn't always keen on working with. While Jane was a brilliant and productive employee, she carried a lot of anger in her heart and often lashed out randomly at any coworker who happened to be nearby. I came to dread our interactions.

One day it was my turn to be on the receiving end of her verbal attacks. I felt both shock and anger as she verbally laid into me but instead of getting into a yelling match with her, I quickly left her office and walked straight to find my boss, Marie. I asked Marie about the situation with Jane and how to handle these verbal outbursts. All Marie would tell me is that Jane came from a very, very challenging childhood and was working on her issues with a therapist. While her episodes of rage were improving, we all had to figure out our own best ways of dealing with these situations. I didn't think that was much to go on at first, but then I took time to think more deeply about Jane.

She obviously had not been raised in a loving, supportive household so expected people to "communicate" through anger and raised voices. Jane may not have received much love, either, and realizing that made my heart melt. Feeling empathy and compassion for her helped me change my approach. Instead of avoiding her, whenever possible I put her in a position to feel confident and be an expert by asking for her advice and experience. I made sure to express my genuine gratitude, too. And the next time Jane started lashing out, I simply stood without reacting and tried to exude peace and love as much as possible. As challenging as that was to pull off (my instincts told me to leave), it worked. While we never became best friends, I am grateful that Jane was one of the people who helped prepare meals for me as I recovered from my traumatic accident that led to my first NDE.

Today's Prayer: *Spirit, thank you for helping me to understand that a little bit of You resides inside the hearts of everyone around me.*

One thing I am grateful for this morning:

Remember to be love. When you go into a difficult situation, take a moment to breathe and get focused on bringing love and light. You can be a source of kindness and compassion with your loving presence.

End Your Day

What I am grateful for today:

What didn't go so well today?

What did I learn from that?

Good stuff that happened:

How can I make tomorrow better?

(Day 7) Begin Your Day: _____

The path to an awakened life of peace and love is often a gradual process. It can start with a desire for a change that comes quietly, growing gently but with strength and purpose. Sometimes we go through challenging events and realize that we want something different for ourselves, so we begin our quest more intentionally, with a strong desire for a more expansive life. Other times, though, that path to peace, love, and awakening may be thrust upon us out of the blue, seemingly without our consent. In these cases, we are forced to confront the new truth: that life, and indeed reality, may be very different from what we thought it was before that moment. In either case, whether we choose the path gently or the path chooses us, walking that path of light and love involves a beautiful, lifelong journey back to the sacred.

Unlike most other journeys, this sacred path to light and awakening never ends. As we learn, grow, and evolve, so too does the path. And as the path evolves, it then prompts us to expand our awareness even more. It is a never-ending cycle. I think of it as a multidimensional spiral path. Some simply call it the Spiral Path, a journey of ever-expanding love, connection, and awareness.

Exploring the depths of Divine love in ourselves, in others, and in this world can be the start of a beautiful adventure all its own.

Today's Prayer: *Spirit, I desire to align myself more fully to your love. Please walk with me and surround me in your loving support.*

One thing I am grateful for this morning:

Today I Intend to:

 Challenge: Create your own heartfelt prayer today. You can use it at any time in addition to, or instead of, the prayers I suggest in this book.

End Your Day

What I am grateful for today:

What didn't go so well today?

What did I learn from that?

Good stuff that happened:

How can I make tomorrow better?

Divine love is the basis of everything, both in this physical world and in the realm of the spiritual.

Week One Review

Use these two pages to summarize your week. What did you experience or learn? Did you have any insights or aha moments? What went well? What would you like more of?

Within diversity lies Beauty. It is our differences that make us beautiful!

Week Two: Love Yourself

Welcome to week two. The first week, devoted to love in general and Divine love more specifically, should have helped you get an idea of how the rest of our time together will flow.

Week two is devoted to helping you begin to recognize that you are worthy of your own love, respect, compassion, and kindness. In my experience, this lesson of learning to genuinely love and care for yourself might seem challenging, bringing up feelings from the past that you thought were long gone.[5]

If the idea of extending love to yourself seems too much of a stretch right now, think about it instead as extending kindness, compassion, or consideration *back to you*, just like you would to someone you dearly love.

My hope is that you begin to form a habit of being loving and kind to yourself on a daily basis, even in small ways. Self-love doesn't mean just allowing yourself to sit on the couch all day, every day, and eat junk food though. It means supporting yourself to be the best *you* that you can be in this moment. Sometimes you *will* need to sit on the couch and watch a fun movie, take a walk, meditate, or pray in order to decompress from a challenging day. Other days you may have to remind yourself of your dreams and goals, and get real with why you are fearful of them, or avoiding them altogether.

How you extend kindness, compassion, and love to yourself will change over the course of your life. It will deepen, expand, and shift depending on your stage of life, level of spiritual and emotional awareness, and the challenges you currently face. Ultimately, I would love for you to be your own most vocal cheerleader, encouraging yourself to reach for your dreams and goals, giving yourself kindness and compassion as you need it, and celebrating your achievements along the way.

---

[5] If that's the case for you, I would encourage you to work on these feelings and memories with a professional counselor. Helping you through these types of challenges is beyond the scope of this book. You deserve to feel happy, positive, and hopeful and a professional therapist can help.

(Day 8) Begin Your Day: _____

"What do you feed your body? How do you keep your mind bright and youthful? Caring for yourself is a way to gift love, kindness, and compassion back on *you*.

"One excellent way to show your gratitude for the life that you have is to treat yourself well. Learn to love and respect your body by drinking clean water, eating healthy foods, getting the right amount of exercise for you, and spending time in the fresh air and sunshine.

"Spirit wants you to enjoy your life. Go for a walk, a run, or a bicycle ride to revel in movement. Swim in a clean lake and enjoy the feel of the cool water. Stand on the top of a hill or mountain and throw your arms back in celebration of life. Love your body with fun, healthy, and challenging experiences. Feed your brain with positive books, media, movies, and information. Try to avoid things that distress your mind because they also stress your body. Love your brain with challenging, new experiences, good people, and healthy hobbies and habits." (AFTL, Chapter 7)

Today's Prayer: *Spirit, thank you for the gift of this life, and the gift of me..*

One thing I am grateful for this morning:

Today I Intend to:

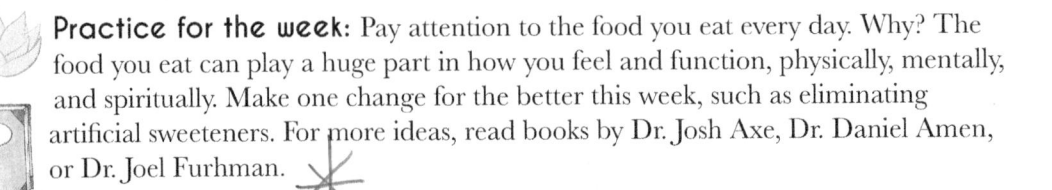

Practice for the week: Pay attention to the food you eat every day. Why? The food you eat can play a huge part in how you feel and function, physically, mentally, and spiritually. Make one change for the better this week, such as eliminating artificial sweeteners. For more ideas, read books by Dr. Josh Axe, Dr. Daniel Amen, or Dr. Joel Furhman.

Extra Credit: Set aside one day per week as a "no media" day. During that one day, completely avoid recreational media (TV, movies, internet) and social media of all kinds. Instead, reconnect with family and friends in a more personal way, or make time for one of your own non-media interests or passions.

End Your Day

What I am grateful for today:

What didn't go so well today?

What did I learn from that?

Good stuff that happened:

How can I make tomorrow better?

(Day 9) Begin Your Day: _____

You are a creative, miraculous person, just as you are right now. You are truly special, beloved, and have gifts that you can share with others. In being *you*, you have the ability to bring joy and love to yourself and those around you. You are creative in a way that is special and unique.

You have your own creative voice, your own song. Share it with the world.

Today's Prayer: *Spirit, today I put myself in alignment with Divine love and creativity so that I can more fully embrace the beautiful person I am.*

One thing I am grateful for this morning:

Today I intend to:

💡 **Your individual, inner light of love is beautiful.** Simply *be* the light, creativity, and love that is yours. Don't be afraid to share it with the world.

Extra Credit: Go back to the "Before You Begin" section section on page 12 and look at what inspires or energizes you. Make an effort to incorporate one of these into your day today.

End Your Day

What I am grateful for today:

What didn't go so well today?

What did I learn from that?

Good stuff that happened:

How can I make tomorrow better?

(Day 10) Begin Your Day: _____

Words hold energy and power whether you speak them aloud to others or silently to yourself. What words do you use when you speak to yourself on a daily basis? This is your inner monologue or "self-talk."

Your self-talk can have an incredible amount of power in your life. You can lift yourself up or tear yourself apart with the words you direct inward. Pay attention to your inner monologue today. Then get real and ask yourself if you would say these same things aloud to the most beloved person in your life. Bringing your awareness to your self-talk will help you begin to adjust the words that you use so that they support you and help you achieve your dreams and goals.

Today's Prayer: *Divine Spirit, I ask that you help me use my words wisely today, for myself and others.*

One thing I am grateful for this morning:

Today I Intend to:

Challenge: Be conscious of your self-talk today, also known as your internal monologue. Write down some of the things that you say to yourself. Being conscious of your self-talk is the first step in making a change for the better. Make note of some of this self-talk here, then ask yourself if you would say these things to your best friend:

Extra Credit: This week, create something that embodies how you view your uniqueness. It could be a sketch, painting, sculpture, song, collage, or anything else you can dream up. But whatever medium you choose, dive into and express the unique energy of *you* in the moment.

End Your Day

What I am grateful for today:

What didn't go so well today?

What did I learn from that?

Good stuff that happened:

How can I make tomorrow better?

(Day 11) Begin Your Day: _____

Are you challenged by the concept of self-love, or have trouble feeling compassion and kindness for yourself? Try focusing on helping other people first.

During my NDE I learned how important it is to surround ourselves in love, compassion, and kindness. But as easy as that may sound, for some people self-love can feel too challenging. But you can work on self-love and compassion from two angles: try to extend love to yourself first (the "inward" method), or begin by focusing on others first (the "outward" method), eventually coming back to yourself.

What do I mean by focusing outward first?

By *outward* I mean spending time helping others in compassionate ways. Volunteer for a cause that tugs at your heart, something that perhaps even brings a tear to your eye when you think about it. Avoid just sending money off to a charity and then going back to your life. Instead, change things up and *tithe with your time*. Charities often need volunteers just as much as they need money. And while you are there volunteering, open up your heart to deeply connect with those whom you serve.

Whether it be at a food bank, hospice, or an animal shelter, take the opportunity to look at everyone around you and realize that you are gazing on aspects of Spirit. Those souls in front of you are a part of the Divine whether they are homeless men and women at the food bank, an elderly couple who needs meals delivered to their home, or even a puppy at the animal shelter. They are all worthy of your love and compassion because they sparkle with Divine light. Then think about the fact that *you* carry that same Divine light, too.

Perhaps one day you'll notice your own reflection in the mirror and see an aspect of Spirit looking back at you, just like those beautiful souls at the food bank. And maybe, just maybe, to that reflection you will be able to send out a little bit of compassion and love.

Today's Prayer: *Spirit, I am ready to let go of anything that is blocking me from living my best, most love-filled life.*

One thing I am grateful for this morning:

Optional journaling exercise: Is there something that you have always wanted to do, such as write a novel or learn photography, but have convinced yourself that you do not have the time to pursue it? Get real with yourself by analyzing your day. Track your activities and time spent on them. Be honest by also jotting down whether it needs to be done or not, and how much joy or fulfillment the activity brings you. Next, consider what you can trade out so that you can pursue that longstanding dream. Remember, making a dream into reality usually takes regular, dedicated time. What do you *really* want? To read stories about everyone else's lives on social media, or truly live *your* life, accomplishing your goals as a unique individual? Making time for your desires and goals is one of the best gifts you can give yourself.

End Your Day

What I am grateful for today:

What didn't go so well today?

What did I learn from that?

Good stuff that happened:

How can I make tomorrow better?

(Day 12) Begin Your Day: _____

Sometimes it is easier to learn self-love if we receive love from someone else, first.

A few months after I recovered from my traumatic accident and NDE, I struggled with trying to figure out how to embrace the teachings of self-love. I simply did not love myself and had no idea how I could make that happen.

Then my intuition led me to visit a horse sanctuary several hours from my home. I signed up for a paid tour to photograph some of their horses, and they paired me with my tour guide, John. We set out across the sanctuary in an old sport utility vehicle (SUV).

After photographing some Spanish Mustangs, John asked if I wanted to take a different path to see a herd of horses that most visitors and volunteers don't usually have the chance to see. I agreed and we drove until we spied the herd John had in mind: a group of horses who were rescued from severe abuse in another state. While they were still a long way off, John cut the engine to see if they would approach us on their own. Over several minutes they wandered to within fifty feet of the vehicle; close enough for me to snap some photos, then they wandered off again. I felt grateful for even a few minutes with them since these beautiful horses rarely trusted anyone.

But John continued to wait for one other horse. A little white mare who had suffered some of the worst abuse imaginable was in this area too, and he hoped that we could spot her. Eventually we caught a glimpse of her, far up a hill, so we waited to see if she would approach. John fully expected the little mare to wander away since she was one of the most elusive horses in the sanctuary.

After watching us for a few minutes, the white mare did something completely unexpected. She began to walk, then trot, directly toward my side of the SUV. My window was already rolled down for photos but she was quickly too close for pictures. As she approached, the abuse on her beautiful skin became apparent. Her white hair was crisscrossed with black scars of all sizes. Not much of her body escaped the punishing blows her former owner inflicted on her. Even her neck and face bore those scars. Tears welled in my eyes. How could anyone treat an animal so poorly?

Then she did something that *really* made me cry. She walked as close to my window as she could and eased her big, beautiful head into the SUV, closed her eyes, and rested her face against me. Call me crazy, but I thought I could feel her love and trust for me enveloping my whole heart. I gently reached up and stroked her head and neck as my tears flowed. She obviously wanted to make a heart-connection with me, to let me know that I was loved. It worked.

We bonded like that for several minutes and shared a spiritual connection that I still cannot put into words. Then with a little snort she pulled her head back, swished her tail a few times, and walked off to join the rest of her little herd.

The whole encounter left me speechless but it did something else too. That little mare helped me open my heart to my own center of love. If she could extend love and trust to me, after all she had been through, how could I not be open to loving myself?

Contemplate for yourself if there someone in your life who could help you see the beautiful person you are.

Today's Prayer: *Spirit, how can I learn to love myself more fully?*

End Your Day

What I am grateful for today:

What didn't go so well today?

What did I learn from that?

Good stuff that happened:

How can I make tomorrow better?

Extra Credit: Go back to the "Before You Begin" section on page 13 and reach out and connect with someone on your "People I love" list.

(Day 13) Begin Your Day: _____

"Take some time to appreciate this gift of a body that you have. You are a glorious being. Billions of cells of different types come together in you and, for the majority of the time, work pretty well to give you this time on Earth. You don't have to think about your cells functioning in order to stay alive. Your body tends to go about the daily aspects of living without much intervention from you. You breathe, your heart beats, and you digest your food without thought. Most of the time, your physical wounds heal with little help. Your body just knows how to heal. You get a scrape or scratch, and in about ten days, new skin has formed and the scrape is gone. If you break a bone, you might have it set but after that your body starts to knit the broken pieces back together, sometimes with the healed bone being stronger than it was before the break. You don't have to think, 'Heal, heal, heal' every day. Your body just does it." (AFTL, Chapter 7)

Today's Prayer: *Spirit, thank you for the gift of my body, and for keeping me in alignment with health and well-being.*

One thing I am grateful for this morning:

Today I Intend to:

Take a moment to **jot down five interesting things** that most people do not know about you. Don't be shy! Write them down here:

Check In: How are you feeling, physically, emotionally, and spiritually?

End Your Day

What I am grateful for today:

What didn't go so well today?

What did I learn from that?

Good stuff that happened:

How can I make tomorrow better?

(Day 14) Begin Your Day: _____

"Love is at the core of your Self. Following the path of love will lead you to many wonders, from becoming one with the beauty of a flower to recognizing that you are a true part of the Divine, and a divine member of this amazing universe." (MFH)

Today's Prayer: *Spirit, thank you for helping me turn away from negativity, and toward love.*

One thing I am grateful for this morning:

Today I Intend to:

Contemplate and note ways that you can show love and appreciation to yourself, then choose one to implement for the rest of this program:

End Your Day

What I am grateful for today:

What didn't go so well today?

What did I learn from that?

Good stuff that happened:

How can I make tomorrow better?

Extra Credit:
Make time to have some fun today.

Week Two Review

Use these two pages to summarize your week. What did you experience or learn? Did you have any insights or aha moments? What went well? What would you like more of?

> Right here, right now, this is a part of heaven.

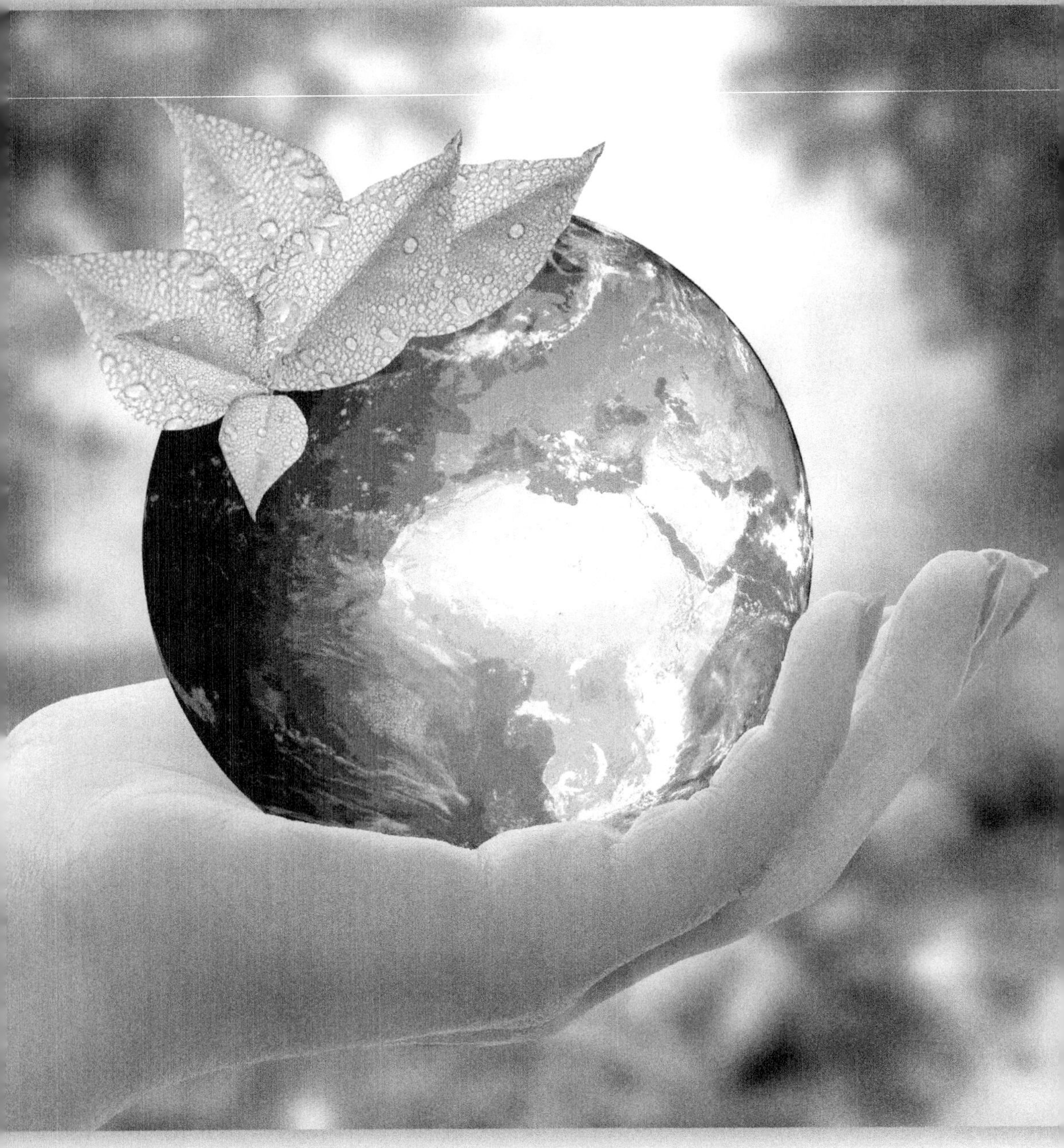

Week Three: Love the Earth

Congratulations on all of the work you have done so far. Give yourself some kudos for making time for yourself over the past two weeks.

Let's continue by considering ways we can better love this little planet we all call home. Never before over the course of the past five thousand (or more) years of our human civilizations has our planet been at such an important yet critical point. The growth of the human population has brought our numbers to almost eight billion people, as of 2021. Combining our population and its resource needs with astounding advances in technology and medical science have brought most of us to a state where we are highly connected and controlled, yet our physical and emotional wellbeing is, paradoxically, beginning to suffer. What is perhaps tougher to overcome is that the environment in which we live is increasingly unhealthy due to our own actions.

I do not condemn our desire for technological and medical advancements. Where would we be without modern healthcare, vaccines, electricity, and computers? But technological achievement needs to be coupled with even bigger advances in morals, ethics, and spirituality if we are to prosper as a species while also allowing other life on this planet to thrive. We must move past our society's outdated view that nothing we do has any consequences.

The reality is that *everything we do affects the world around us.*

Technology alone cannot carry our society into a healthy and sustainable future — only by growing our emotional and spiritual maturity at the same time can we evolve into a civilization that takes responsibility for itself and its effects on the planet. These are lessons we all need to learn, the sooner the better.

You can have a positive impact on the planet just by making some small (ish) adjustments to the way you live your daily life. You might not think that changing a few minor habits, like taking a shorter shower, using bio-based soaps and shampoos, or switching your omega-3 supplement, could have much of an effect on the health of the environment. After all, you are just one person out of billions. But your actions *do* count. Each choice you make to live more consciously and in tune with the health of the planet makes a difference. Even more important is the example that you are setting for others: your children, your friends, your neighbors, and your community.

Every person making more conscious and loving choices, matters.

Your choices make a difference.

(Day 15) Begin Your Day:_____

"The natural world is a tremendous gift. It sustains and nourishes us. We are utterly dependent on it for our survival. We have no other place within our solar system, or even the physical universe, that we can call home. When we feel gratitude for this gift, we send a message of love and appreciation back to Spirit for what we've been given.

"We have but one world, and but one chance to love, cherish, and enjoy it as the people we are now. More importantly, our children and grandchildren will have only one chance as well — what legacy do we want to leave for them?

"Our actions today can have a profound effect on those who will come after us." (AFTL, Chapter 8)

Today's Prayer: *Spirit, thank you for the gift of this amazing planet we call home.*

One thing I am grateful for this morning:

Today I intend to be kind to the Earth by:

Practice for the week: Think about ways that you can decrease your consumption of processed foods and move toward a more organic, sustainable diet. Then implement at least one of them this week. Reducing the consumption of processed foods and moving toward whole, organic foods not only helps improve your health, it helps the health of the planet too. Why? Processing takes more energy and resources than eating foods in their more natural states. Processing foods also (usually) introduces more chemicals, sugars, and allergens than would normally be present in the whole food alone.

Extra Credit: Go back to the "Before You Begin" section on page 13 and review your "I Want to Learn" list. Choose one of them and take a step toward learning it this week. Locate a book, website, or class that will get you started.

End Your Day

What I am grateful for today:

What didn't go so well today?

What did I learn from that?

Good stuff that happened:

How can I make tomorrow better?

(Day 16) Begin Your Day: _____

Not too many years ago, my then eleven year old daughter, Michelle, and I were walking in a wildlife refuge near Tacoma, Washington. An autumn chill hung in the air that October day, and the cold prompted droves of wooly bear caterpillars to scramble *en masse* to find places to hibernate for the winter.

The little caterpillars felt the need to crawl across the refuge's main path. Maybe there was a particularly good thicket of shrubs on one side that would give them shelter for the winter, or perhaps they were just following some unspoken instinct to crawl in a particular direction. But unfortunately for the wooly bears, the walking path they needed to cross teemed with people all day. Many of the caterpillars didn't make it across the path because most of the walkers were not paying attention to what was happening on the ground beneath their feet.

Michelle took one look at the caterpillars, then at the feet of all of those people, and sprung into action. She began picking up the caterpillars and moving them to the shrubs along the side of the path so that they would survive to continue their journeys.

This may not seem like a big deal but Michelle knew without a doubt it was the right thing to do, so we both spent the next hour or more moving caterpillars from the path to the shrubs. But here is the most magical part of the story: by watching Michelle, other adults and kids on the path became conscious of the caterpillars and went out of their way to avoid stepping on them. Some even stopped to help us. Soon we had a platoon of adults and children helping move caterpillars off the busy walking path.

I am very proud of my daughter for being unabashedly herself: for caring about the little critters that most people ignore, and for quietly being a model to others with her actions, helping them to become more conscious of the natural world.

Did Michelle save the world that day? No, but she did save some cute, fuzzy caterpillars. More importantly, though, her actions caused other people to become conscious of their own effects on the natural world around them. In the end, it was this ripple effect of her actions that made the biggest, longest-lasting impact.

Remember that we are connected to everyone and everything on Earth, even the lowly wooly bear caterpillar, and every action we take has an impact on the world around us.

Today's Prayer: *Today, I intend to walk in peace and light, and with respect for all of the other creatures on this beautiful little planet I call home.*

One thing I am grateful for this morning:

Today I Intend to:

End Your Day

What I am grateful for today:

What didn't go so well today?

What did I learn from that?

Good stuff that happened:

How can I make tomorrow better?

> ***Extra Credit:*** This week, create something that embodies how you view our planet or the natural world. It could be a sketch, painting, sculpture, song, or anything else you can dream up. But whatever medium you choose, dive into and express your unique energy in the moment.

(Day 17) Begin Your Day: _____

"Nature has always been my home and refuge. I see it as an entity in its own right, deserving of respect and love just as we humans are. Without its life-giving water, oxygen, and soils, we wouldn't be here. We cannot survive without the natural world, plain and simple.

"My personal ethic has been to love and respect the Earth and all of its inhabitants. But since coming close to losing my own life, and experiencing some form awakening, I seem to be developing something deeper — a profound sense of reverence.

"Reverence means to have deep respect, awe, and even veneration for something. When I say I revere the Earth, what does that mean in my own life? My *needs* are getting simpler and less materialistic all of the time. I still use paper, drive a car, and take vacations, but I minimize my consumption. I also harbor a deep feeling of gratitude for what we have here on this small planet, for the gift we've been given in this Earth. It really is our small life raft in a vast universe of inhospitable places. I minimize my impact by using less, buying fewer "toys," being OK with an older car, recycling, encouraging organic farming by purchasing local and organically grown food, and donating time and money to conservation organizations. I also feel driven to write about nature and, through my writing, art, and speaking, help others see the beauty in this beautiful place we all call *home*." (AFTL, Chapter 8)

Today's Prayer: *Spirit, help me find ways to show more care and reverence to the Earth.*

One thing I am grateful for this morning:

Today I Intend to:

Challenge: Watch a beautiful nature documentary this week, one that inspires you or gives you insights that you have not had before. Then consider at least one thing you can do to help the natural world.

End Your Day

What I am grateful for today:

What didn't go so well today?

What did I learn from that?

Good stuff that happened:

How can I make tomorrow better?

(Day 18) Begin Your Day: _____

The moment I drove into the Redwood forest of northern California, emotion flooded over me and tears began to gather in my eyes. I felt as if I were coming home to family somehow, which was strange because this was my first time visiting this place, at least in this life. I was in my late forties, coming home to a place that I'd never been before like the John Denver song, "Rocky Mountain High." Only this was California, not Colorado.

I first stopped at the Grove of the Titans and yes, this group of trees lived up to its name. Exiting my car, I wandered among them, awed by their size, majesty, and *presence*. Single trees twenty feet across or more towered over 275 feet tall. I stood in the middle of hundreds of natural, living skyscrapers whose heights could dwarf a 25 story building. But unlike the city with its concrete and steel where I always felt alien and hemmed-in, here I felt welcomed, at peace, and somehow *at home*.

These giants were living, breathing sentinels of time and life. Some individual trees had been here for more than 2,000 years, quietly anchoring the coastal hills. When I stilled my own mind I thought I could sense their slow, measured conversations with each other. These were just trees, right? How could they be communicating? But scientists are beginning to find that these titans of the plant world are conscious beings as well, as in fact are *all* plants. Their consciousness differs from yours and mine, definitely, but they are conscious nonetheless. And in my heart and soul, I felt as though these giant trees were extending their friendship to me.

These trees are sacred, too, not just to me but also to the Earth and somehow to the realm of Spirit. I felt it deep in my bones, the sacredness of this hallowed ground. The Redwoods had the feeling and presence of the heavenly realm I visited during my near-death experience, and I almost expected my spiritual Guide to step out from behind one of the towering trunks to continue my lessons.

Today's Prayer: *Spirit, thank you for the life-giving nature of this beautiful planet.*

One thing I am grateful for this morning:

Today I Intend to:

Optional exercise: Do you feel a connection with nature? If so, how? If not, why not? What are your favorite places in nature? Think about ways that you can incorporate a little bit more of the natural world into your life. Perhaps take a walk in a park, go to the beach, or stare at the moon on a clear night. Journal about your connection to nature, draw a picture, or craft a song if you would like to add a little more heart-based energy to this exercise.

End Your Day

What I am grateful for today:

What didn't go so well today?

What did I learn from that?

Good stuff that happened:

How can I make tomorrow better?

Extra Credit: Go back to the "Before You Begin" section on page 12 and review your "Inspires/Energizes Me" list. Choose one topic or activity to incorporate into your week.

(Day 19) Begin Your Day:

"Modern science is demonstrating the interconnectedness of Earth's ecosystems. An event that happens in one place can greatly impact another part of the Earth. A simple example is heavy downpours of rain can cause a river to flood, inundating farms and wetlands for hundreds of miles downstream. That same overflow of water can bring valuable minerals and nutrients to the wetlands where the river meets the sea, enriching the plant life that feeds the animals, and us.

"We are also intimately connected with all of nature. It gives us life. We are dependent on nature for our survival. To mistreat it is, in the end, to mistreat ourselves. If we pollute a waterway with untreated waste from our chemical plants, where does that pollution go? It eventually gets back into us through the very water we drink and the food we eat. Does this mean we're not supposed to live, eat, and breathe?

"No. But it does mean that we do the best we can to protect what we have and use it wisely. We can aim to have as little negative impact as possible on our immediate environment and the planet. It also means that we try to make things better when and where we can, to the best of our abilities."

None of us are comic book superheroes, able to save the world all on our own, but if we each do what we can, it will add up to something big. (AFTL, Chapter 8)

Today's Prayer: *Spirit, thank you for helping me live more harmoniously on this Earth and with all of its citizens.*

One thing I am grateful for this morning:

Today I Intend to:

As you eat your meals today, take a few moments to **contemplate the source of your food.** If you eat a salad for lunch, think about where the vegetables originated. Contemplate the soil that grew the vegetables, the water that hydrated the plants, and the sunshine that helped the lettuce grow. Consider the bounty the Earth gives you every day, and take a moment to feel gratitude for it.

End Your Day

What I am grateful for today:

What didn't go so well today?

What did I learn from that?

Good stuff that happened:

How can I make tomorrow better?

(Day 20) Begin Your Day: _____

"During my NDE, the sights, sounds, and feelings of the spiritual realm were amazing, no doubt about it. But what we have here on Earth is no less wonderful. Whales sing in our beautiful oceans, mountains soar taller and grander than any skyscraper, beautiful beaches beckon us to relax, and prairies where the sky seems to go on forever show us humility. The Earth itself nourishes us with abundant crops to eat, air to breathe, water to drink, and fibers with which to clothe ourselves."

Take some time right now to consider what the Earth gives you every day. (AFTL, Chapter 8)

Today's Prayer: *Spirit, thank you for helping us all experience, celebrate, and protect this planet to the best of our abilities.*

One thing I am grateful for this morning:

Today I Intend to:

Consider this: One easy way to **save money and conserve energy** is to set your home's thermostat to a warmer temperature setting in the summer and a cooler one in the winter.

Extra Credit: Would you like to help the planet in a more direct way? Research environmental charities to which you can donate time or money. Some of my favorites are The Nature Conservancy and local wildlife rescue and rehabilitation centers.

End Your Day

What I am grateful for today:

What didn't go so well today?

What did I learn from that?

Good stuff that happened:

How can I make tomorrow better?

(Day 21) Begin Your Day: _____

Some ways that you can be kind to the planet:
1) Realize that true happiness, joy, and peace do not come from the stuff you own.
2) Buy organic produce when you can, especially from farms local to you. You'll get better-quality food, and lessen the pollution that comes with chemical pesticides and fertilizers.
3) To reset your perspective on how much stuff you actually require in order to live, volunteer at a homeless shelter, a refugee camp, or in a developing country.
4) Eat more (organic) plants and less meat. You might even lose weight and feel better while you reduce your impact on the planet.
5) Practice gratitude for what you do have. It may help you realize just how blessed you actually are!
6) If you need something, buy it (gently) used if you can.
7) Understand that the Earth is the *only* planet on which our species can survive.

Today's Prayer: *Spirit, how can I live more lightly on this planet?*

One thing I am grateful for this morning:

Do you want a quick way to contribute to a healthier planet? Change your use of omega-3 supplements. Move toward vegan sources of omega-3s and away from fish and krill. No matter what you hear from supplement companies who have a vested financial interest in "greenwashing" you, the human consumption of krill and wild caught ocean-going fish is not sustainable at our current numbers. This is especially true for krill. **You do not need krill. Whales do.** Whales cannot visit the local grocery story and find something else to eat. You can. Every time you consume krill products, you are literally taking food from the mouths of the great whales and other marine life that depends on this tiny but important critter. **No amount of human consumption of krill is sustainable.** Good alternatives are omega-3 supplements made from algae, or consuming a variety of other vegan sources (flax seeds, hemp seeds, walnuts, etc.).

End Your Day

What I am grateful for today:

What didn't go so well today?

What did I learn from that?

Good stuff that happened:

How can I make tomorrow better?

Week Three Review:

Use these two pages to summarize your week. What did you experience or learn? Did you have any insights or aha moments? What went well? What would you like more of?

Focus on what **CAN** accomplish in this moment, not on what you can't.

Week Four: Creativity

What does creativity mean to you? Do you think it is something that only artists, musicians, and inventors can access, or is it available to anyone?

Creativity is actually something we *all* share. At its most basic, it is the ability to bring something new into existence such as creating a piece of art, building a kitchen table, or designing the next, most advanced computer chip. But creativity is so much more than the creation of *stuff*. In its higher forms, it is the ability to craft something totally new based on a myriad of prior ideas put together in new ways, coupled with out-of-the-box thinking and maybe even Divine inspiration.

What contributes to this higher level of creativity, when abstract concepts are made real? Personal experience and education help. In order to make advances in the field of physics, for example, it often helps to know what came before. It also helps to have an innately curious and questioning nature (why *can't* we reuse a rocket or create a modern electric car), the resources (time and/or money) to devote to experimentation and play, the ability or desire to daydream, and passion for the project. But I believe something more is required if we want to access the highest levels of creativity: a more conscious connection to Spirit and the universe, which can be cultivated through practices such as the ones I share this book.

Creativity is not only for artistic geniuses like Leonardo da Vinci, Ludwig von Beethoven, or Alex Haley. Each day that you are here on this planet, you make choices that help you create and shape your future. *Each choice you make is act of creation.* You create your future with the choices you make today.

This week, I hope that you become more aware of these choices and at the same time begin to learn how to use them to create the life of your dreams. I also invite you to draw, paint, sculpt, knit, sew, dance, or create music that reflects what you feel or comes to you as insights or inspiration this week. Give free reign to your creativity! I would love to see what comes from your heart (and art).

Consider keeping a notebook with you at all times, either an actual book or a file on your mobile device. Jot down anything creative that pops into your mind. Examples could include an idea for a new business, a vision for piece of artwork, or even snippets of a novel you're considering writing. Committing your ideas to paper or an electronic file gives them the respect they deserve, plus you'll be able to review them periodically and implement the ones that call out to you.

(Day 22) Begin Your Day: _____

"Using your creativity, you have the power to bring something into reality that has never before existed: a painting, a piece of music, a beautiful building, an idea that brings peace or understanding, an app, a new medical breakthrough, even a baby's new life. All start with a spark of creativity, inspiration, or imagination. The power that you have to create is immense. You should not take it or yourself lightly.

"You are an amazing and powerful person, whether you believe it or not. Whatever fears or insecurities you have, at your core is creativity and power. Your real power doesn't come from ruling countries or controlling everyone around you, though. It comes from your own creative spark, your thoughts, what is in your heart, the decisions you make, and the interactions you have with other people. When all of these factors work together in harmony and love, you can accomplish almost anything." (AFTL, Chapter 9)

Today's Prayer: *Today my desire and intent is to live from a place of strength and creativity, in alignment with the greatest and highest good for all.*

One thing I am grateful for this morning:

Today I Intend to:

Practice for the week: Easy negativity fasting. To live more peacefully and rid yourself of the negative chatter of the modern world while creating space for creativity and Divine inspiration, it is important to monitor the media that you allow into your life. Avoid negative news and messaging in video and audio form this week, including on television networks, social media, podcasts, etc. If you want to stay updated on current events, read the news in a reliable newspaper or online news outlet. Why? Video and audio media can be powerful avenues to manipulate you into an emotional reaction. Also, with network news programs you have little choice about what is being fed to you. You receive programming that is designed to elicit an emotional response, not to actually give you unbiased information. By reading the news rather than watching or hearing it, you have more control over what you take in, and have more time to analyze it for yourself.

End Your Day

What I am grateful for today:

What didn't go so well today?

What did I learn from that?

Good stuff that happened:

How can I make tomorrow better?

Extra Credit: Go back to the "Before You Begin" section on page 12 and review your "Inspires/Energizes Me" list. Choose one topic or activity to incorporate into your week.

(Day 23) Begin Your Day: _____

Since my accident and first near-death experience, my art and creativity have changed considerably. My skills at the craft of painting drastically improved, and I think my style has evolved, too. But my desire to paint has absolutely skyrocketed. I actually *need* to paint now, and in new, different ways. I am no longer content with my old style. Fresh, new concepts are coming to me pretty much continuously as if creative floodgates opened up.

What changed?

I am still not exactly sure. On a purely physical level, I know my traumatic brain injury (TBI) affected my left frontal and temporal lobes, thought to be the center of language and analytical thinking. Sure enough, after my accident I had a lot of trouble with reading, math, remembering names, speaking, and computer programming. I was a strongly verbal thinker prior to my accident. Today, I think mostly in pictures and concepts, and have to translate those into words so that I can communicate with everyone else. Perhaps the brain injury had something to do with change in the way I create art.

On a more spiritual level, though, I think that being put directly in touch with Spirit during my death on the operating table deeply changed me, too. How could it not? Beauty and love beyond measure, communication so deep and meaningful that it couldn't be translated into words, and being accepted and celebrated without question for simply who and what I was, both as a human and a soul, changed me. And for that I am grateful. It also forged a stronger connection to my creative, Higher Power. I know that every time I step up to the easel, I am allowing Spirit to flow through me and on to canvas.

And perhaps death allowed me to be fearless, to stop worrying about what others might think. I suspect this is where some of my more recent pieces originate, from this fearlessness. Becoming a more courageous, creative, conceptual, spiritual person, seeing connections rather than separation. Feeling free to creatively channel whatever comes to me. My style continues to evolve into something more contemporary, more imaginative, and incorporating more of the concepts I learned during my NDE. I have a purpose now, too: to celebrate connections, love, and spiritual truth in my art.

Today's Prayer: *I am open to learning how I can make kind, wise, creative choices today and every day.*

One thing I am grateful for this morning:

Optional journaling exercise: Think about your past and present, the decisions you have made, and how those decisions have influenced or created the life you are living today. Then consider what you want your future to look like, and what, if anything, you need to do differently in order to create that future for yourself.

End Your Day

What I am grateful for today:

What didn't go so well today?

What did I learn from that?

Good stuff that happened:

How can I make tomorrow better?

> You are more creative and powerful than you know and imagine.

(Day 24) Begin Your Day: _____

"You have individual, creative gifts that allow you to fully express yourself, your love, and your connection to Divinity in a multitude of ways. You can absolutely tap this creative energy at any time…it is there, just waiting for you to call on it. By accessing it, by expressing this inspired creativity, you are again displaying your love and gratitude for the gifts you were given.

"This doesn't mean that your creative gifts must be artistic like being a painter, musician, writer, or sculptor. You have many avenues available to you to tap into this well of creativity. Perhaps you are a master at restoring old cars or homes; maybe you bake and decorate beautiful cakes; perhaps you are an inspired grade school teacher, floral designer, storyteller, or house painter. Or maybe your creativity lies in solving mathematical problems, engineering a new type of solar panel, or designing sports cars. Your creative power might be in raising loving, healthy children who will go on to be great gifts to all who know them." (AFTL, Chapter 9)

Today's Prayer: *Divine Spirit, allow me to recognize and bring forth the creative being that I am at my core.*

One thing I am grateful for this morning:

Today I Intend to:

Challenge: What talents, interests, or creative inspiration do you have that you are not pursuing? Why? Is there one that you would like to pursue? What is stopping you?

End Your Day

What I am grateful for today:

What didn't go so well today?

What did I learn from that?

Good stuff that happened:

How can I make tomorrow better?

(Day 25) Begin Your Day: _____

"Peace isn't something you find as if it were a pretty shell on a beach. It is something you choose to create. Each choice can contribute to creating peace in your life." (MFH)

Today's Prayer: *Spirit, how can I create a more peace and love in my life?*

One thing I am grateful for this morning:

Today I Intend to:

Starting today, I would love for you to recognize all of the ways that you are creative. Did you have an idea for a new product? Put in a new garden bed or plant a tree, write one more chapter in your book, or strengthen a relationship that has been strained? Jot them down here (alternately, keep a separate notebook dedicated to your creative insights):

Extra Credit: Go back to the "Before You Begin" section on page 13 and reach out and connect with someone on your "People I love" list.

End Your Day

What I am grateful for today:

What didn't go so well today?

What did I learn from that?

Good stuff that happened:

How can I make tomorrow better?

(Day 26) Begin Your Day: _____

Let's take a moment to think about what is commonly known as artistic or inventive creativity. More than just making decisions that shape your future, inventive creativity is often characterized by flashes of insight or solutions to problems that come seemingly out of the blue. Closely related to intuition, this inventive aspect of creativity can be nurtured and enhanced just like any other skill. I cannot promise that you will become another Picasso, but you *can* learn to strengthen this form of creativity and use it to enhance your life.

Spending time in what I call *quiet mind* activities, such as hiking in nature, going for a walk in a park, meditating, praying, gardening, and more, gives your mind and soul the creative space to foster new ideas. It also makes it easier for you to connect with that higher source of insight that you might call Spirit, the universe, God, or even the Akashic Field. Recent research into creativity also demonstrates that spending time in green places (forests, gardens, parks, etc.) also promotes the ability to have creative insights.

For me personally, it helps to take care of all aspects of my health. Avoiding sugar and other junk food, alcohol, and recreational drugs is key. Getting regular exercise and quality sleep also help me feel and function at my best. While I cannot correlate these directly to enhanced creativity, it is tough to focus on being innovative when my body and brain are not functioning well. Taking care of my life (keeping my finances in good shape, living without fear, avoiding drama, avoiding too much network and social media, staying connected with friends), keeps my stress levels low. For me, too much stress saps my artistic creativity because it is hard to focus on painting or writing if my life is in chaos.

One of the world's most creative musicians, Wolfgang A. Mozart, said that his best compositions came to him as he was riding in a carriage and daydreaming (the equivalent to today's cabs or buses). Other people get insights during those moments just before they fall asleep. In those times when we are partly tuned out of everyday life, creative insights can come easily and without much thought. So my suggestion is to make time for daydreaming safely, ride the bus or the train on your next commute, or let a spouse or friend take the wheel on your next road trip together while you, a passenger, let your mind wander.

Finally, one of the most important things you can do is to continually yet gently ask questions of Spirit. "What if," "I wonder why," and "How can I," are great open-ended, creativity-building questions. Then be open and ready for the answers because they can come when you least expect them.

Today's Prayer: *Spirit, how can I* _____?

One thing I am grateful for this morning:

Do you daydream, or spend any time in mind-quieting activities?
Allowing yourself a bit of time each day for your mind to wander or rest has been shown to boost creativity.

End Your Day

What I am grateful for today:

What didn't go so well today?

What did I learn from that?

Good stuff that happened:

How can I make tomorrow better?

(Day 27) Begin Your Day: _____

Creativity isn't only about art, music, or poetry. At its core, it means bringing into existence something that is new. This can even include helping others feel better, such as bringing positivity and light to someone who is feeling down.

One Saturday evening I was shopping at a large, chain, organic grocery store, just buying a few things to make a salad for dinner that night. But honestly, I was not all that interested in eating, having finally ended a three month relationship with a man who simply was not a good fit for me. I guess I wore my sadness on my face as I stepped up to the cash register because the clerk, a young woman in her mid-twenties, took one look at me and said, "Oh, honey, what happened?"

I felt surprised that she had noticed my emotional state. An even bigger surprise was that she cared. She saw hundreds of customers a day so I felt amazed that she had the energy and compassion to notice the sadness of one customer. As I placed my vegetables on the counter, I told her about the breakup.

"It looks like you could use a hug," she said. I nodded and she marched around the checkout counter and gave me the biggest bear hug I had in a long time! I laughed and thanked her as she went back to the register to continue checking me out.

I immediately felt lifted up, more at peace, and hopeful again. All it took was one person to extend a hug of comfort and take a few moments to create a little light in my heart. (*Note: this is a pre-COVID story.*)

Today's Prayer: *How can I live more creatively, in aspects of my life, and in alignment with the greatest and highest good?*

One thing I am grateful for this morning:

Today I Intend to:

Your goal for today: create a little fun for yourself. Modern life is filled with enough tasks that we are compelled to do and may not even enjoy. Carve out at least a few minutes to do something enjoyable for you (as long as it doesn't harm yourself or others).

End Your Day

What I am grateful for today:

What didn't go so well today?

What did I learn from that?

Good stuff that happened:

How can I make tomorrow better?

(Day 28) Begin Your Day: _____

"Your thoughts, words, and actions are forms of energy, and travel out from you as ripples on a pond travel outward from the drop of a pebble on its surface. It doesn't matter whether those thoughts, words, and actions are positive or negative, they still affect the world around you. If a leaf is floating on the surface of that pond, it will move in response to the energy of the ripple that passes under it. It's all energy, radiating out from its source and interacting with all it contacts." (AFTL, Chapter 15)

You have the power to create a more beautiful, kind, loving, and peace-filled world for yourself and your family, every day. Each choice you make and action you take is creation made real, so how will you use this opportunity? Will you create more beauty, connection, compassion, and understanding, or will you bring forth fear and divisiveness? I encourage you to go within your heart, consider what your soul longs for, and then help bring that to fruition by consciously creating it for yourself and your family. Focusing on creating a life of love, beauty, and connection first can be a first step in creating a world that is more living and peace-filled for all.

Today's Prayer: *Spirit, today I joyfully open my heart and mind to living from a place of kindness and creativity.*

One thing I am grateful for this morning:

Today I Intend to:

Make an effort to **be conscious of the words you speak today.** Slow down. Think first. Ask yourself, "Is what I'm about to say kind, compassionate, or helpful?" If not, consider modifying your words. You can get your point across while also being kind.

End Your Day

What I am grateful for today:

What didn't go so well today?

What did I learn from that?

Good stuff that happened:

How can I make tomorrow better?

Week Four Review

Use these two pages to summarize your week. What did you experience or learn? Did you have any insights or aha moments? What went well? What would you like more of?

Don't settle for putting your life on autopilot.
Work toward living the life of your dreams, one step at a time.

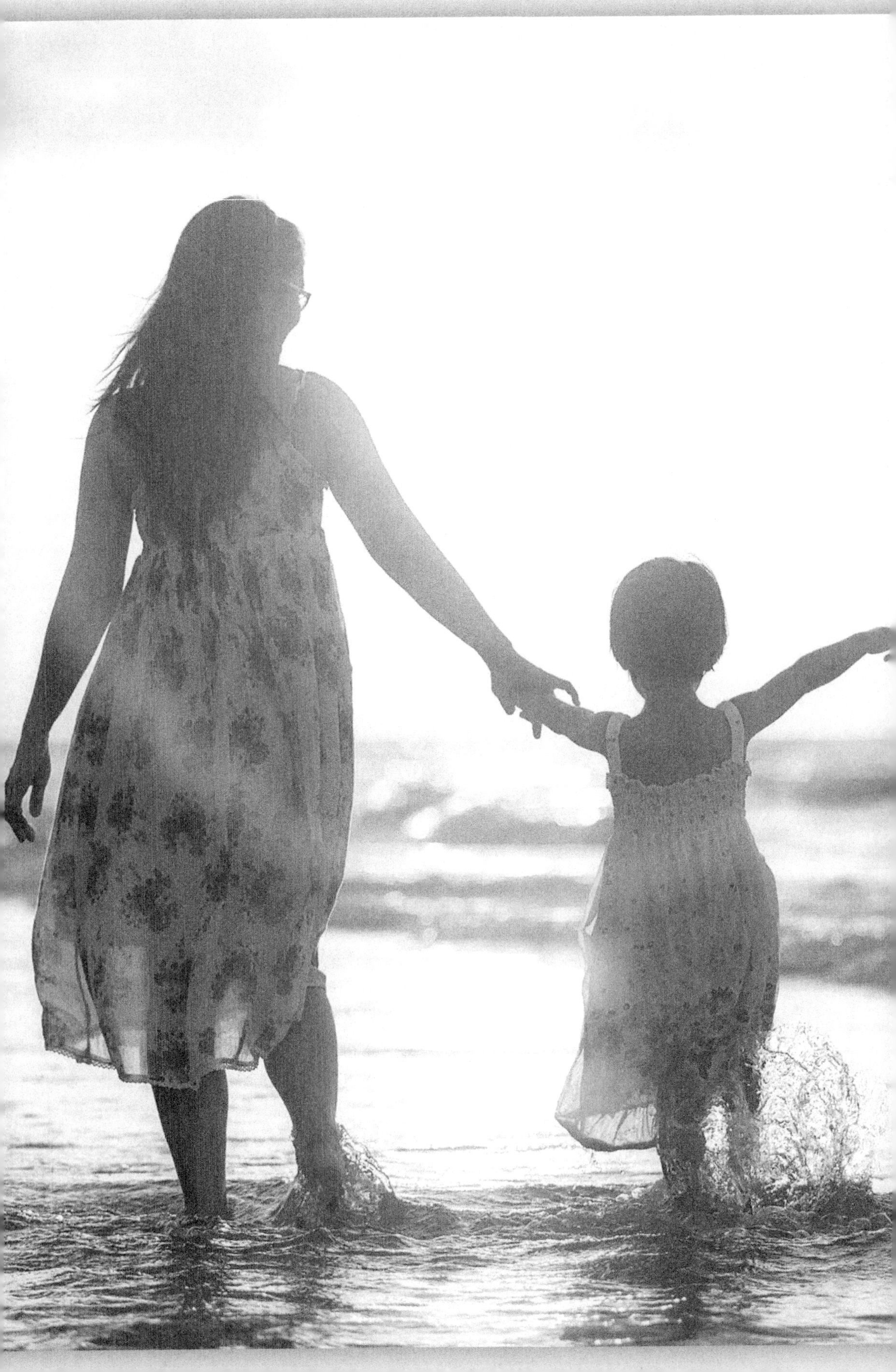

Week Five: Connections

Great job on mastering the basics of the first month of this program! You are now ready to dive into some of the real magic on this path: your connections to others, to the planet, to the universe, and to Spirit.

The topic of learning about your place in the cosmos is huge, so I want to give you a few focused areas to consider as you begin to explore this very sacred and mystical part of life. I will also share a few of my personal, favorite practices that are designed to help you feel a bit more connected to others and the world around you.

Many scientists and spiritually minded people do agree on one basic concept: that we humans are inextricably connected to each other and in fact, to every other being on this planet. I'm going to take it a bit further though: we are intimately connected to our own solar system, to our galaxy and, indeed, the universe as a whole.

How is it possible for these connections to exist?

From the scientific views of the last century or so, our universe came into being from essentially nothing about 14 billion years ago. Time, space, and what we call physical matter did not exist prior to this, or so the story goes. But then somehow, from one minuscule point, all of space, all matter, all that we perceive, and all we cannot yet perceive, and even what we call the passage of time, came into being from a single moment of creation that is still not well understood. At that moment, all that we call *matter* was *one*, and our connections were forged at the very smallest scale. You can read more about this in books by Dr. Travis Taylor and Dr. Brian Greene (see Section 5, "Additional Resources," at the end of this book for more information).

Taking this more scientific perspective, it is reasonable to consider the universe itself to be one huge, single entity. If that bends your mind too much, you can think of it as a single system, similar to how the Pacific Ocean is one large body of water where everything ultimately interacts with everything else. Similarly, as beings on Earth we are one small part of the system of the much larger universe. Bur there is a spiritual aspect to this universal connectedness that we can explore as well, which is the focus for this week.

The most enlightening aspects of my near-death experience (NDE) were the sudden, clear memories I had that what we call physical reality is merely an illusion, at least from the perspective of our spiritual selves. We are energy beings or *souls*, and at the level of our souls' energies we are connected to each other in ways that supersede physical matter. This is the framework of the spiritual level of existence. These spiritual connections bind us to each other, to everything in the universe, and to the Divine.

Let's begin exploring these connections.

(Day 29) Begin Your Day: _____

There is no "here" and "there" when we're talking about the physical and spiritual realms. Both are part of one continuum of existence. What we call the "afterlife" isn't a separate, completely removed *physical* location that your soul travels to when your physical body dies. *Physical* reality is really a part of *spiritual* reality, but they are different energy levels and consciousness states within the same universe.

Everything is interconnected. Everything.

What I call Divine energy or Divine love forms the underlying structure of all that is. Others call this the Divine Field, the Akasha, or Divine Consciousness. It is the basis on which everything is created, both in the physical and spiritual realms.

And since you live in this universe, you are an integral part of this Divine, conscious field of love too.

Today's Prayer: *Spirit, show me how I can be more consciously aware of my part in this grand universe.*

One thing I am grateful for this morning:

Today I Intend to:

Practice for the week: Take time each day to recognize Spirit all around you. When you see someone, take a moment to remember that they are connected to you, and are just as much a part of Spirit as you are. You are both light-filled, spiritual beings having an experience of humanity. In fact, everything around you shares the core energy of Sprit: the animals, plants, insects, mountains, prairies, rivers, and oceans. All are a part of Divine love, as are you.

End Your Day

What I am grateful for today:

What didn't go so well today?

What did I learn from that?

Good stuff that happened:

How can I make tomorrow better?

Check In: How are you feeling, physically, emotionally, and spiritually?

(Day 30) Begin Your Day: _____

"How often have you heard about the concept of "oneness" or interconnectedness of all things? It sounds kind of hippie, doesn't it? People might talk about it within the confines of our religious institutions, and popular spiritual literature today discusses this topic often, yet how many of us actually believe it, practice it, or view life this way?

"During my NDE, I learned that as I looked into the eyes of another human, I was gazing on a part of God. That's one way we can experience Divine connection here on Earth. That Divine presence is a part of the person across the aisle from us when we're on a plane or bus. Spiritual love lives in her heart. Spirit's joy suffuses his soul. And that person you are looking upon is special too, just as you are.

"It is hard for us on Earth to hear or see that spiritual spark inside of others because of our busy-ness, our distractions, and the noise of life. We struggle to notice that someone who annoys or angers us also has a spiritual center, a core of Spirit's presence, just as we ourselves do. But try to remember that in a very real way, we are all connected to each other through our ties to Spirit." (AFTL, Chapter 10)

Today's Prayer: *Spirit, I ask to feel at one with your presence today.*

One thing I am grateful for this morning:

Today I Intend to:

To learn more about oneness from science-based viewpoints, read *Entangled Minds* by Dean Radin, *One Mind* by Larry Dossey, or *The Akashic Experience* by Ervin Laszlo.

Extra Credit: Go back to the "Before You Begin" section (page 13) and review your "I Want to Learn" list. Choose one of them and take a step toward learning it. Locate a book, website, or class that will get you started.

End Your Day

What I am grateful for today:

What didn't go so well today?

What did I learn from that?

Good stuff that happened:

How can I make tomorrow better?

(Day 31) Begin Your Day: _____

Have you ever had one of those weeks where things seemed to be going wrong? Where you didn't see a clear path ahead, or struggled with a seemingly insurmountable decision?

We can get so caught up in our dramas that it's tough to step back and see our lives from a wider perspective. That's when Spirit, our guides, or the angelic realm may decide to help us. We are always connected to them and they know just when to step in.

Normally, challenging events or decisions don't mess with my inner peace anymore. I am usually in a very centered, present place in my mind and soul. But one day not too long ago, I found myself feeling uneasy. Some business opportunities that I thought would be clear and simple to navigate turned out to be confused and uncertain. It felt as though these agreements were about to go up in smoke. Unfortunately I allowed all of the uncertainty to upset my sense of inner peace.

But uncertainty and confusion can hold tremendous gifts.

I decided to take a walk because I connect better with my higher guidance when I'm outside in nature. Before setting off, I asked Spirit and my guides, aloud, to bring clarity to my confusion. I then set out on my walk, not expecting an answer anytime soon.

About twenty minutes later I spied an elderly gentleman walking toward me on the same path. He shuffled slowly but steadily in my direction, head bent down and staring intently at his feet. He didn't seem to notice me at all. Just as we were poised to pass each other, he yanked his gaze up from its focus on his feet, looked me straight in the eye and belted out, "It's all Perfect!"

He then immediately locked his gaze back down to his feet and shuffled away, disappearing behind me. I looked back, half-expecting him to fade away like mist in the sunlight but instead he simply walked around a bend in the path. At least he wasn't a complete figment of my imagination.

But the more I thought about this gentleman and his message, I realized it must have been some kind of intervention from Spirit. It's all perfect. And it was the perfect reminder I needed in order let go and allow events to unfold on their own.

Today's Prayer: *Spirit, help me recognize and strengthen the love that ties me to the rest of the world, and to You.*

One thing I am grateful for this morning:

Remember to feel and express gratitude to the people you encounter today. Gratitude is a form of love so in expressing it, you strengthen positive, loving connections not only to those around you, but to your spiritual Source as well.

End Your Day

What I am grateful for today:

What didn't go so well today?

What did I learn from that?

Good stuff that happened:

How can I make tomorrow better?

> Love is a blessing, the core energy that ties us all together. It calls out across time and space.

(Day 32) Begin Your Day: _____

Message from Nancy's spiritual guides:

"If each one of you realized the magnitude of the connections that exist just among your kind [humanity], you would never raise a hand in violence against each other again. Think about these connections as if they were a giant, multidimensional, gossamer web of energy: if you destroy just one strand of a web, you weaken the whole structure. In reverse, you can strengthen the web of these loving connections by reinforcing one strand at a time. Focus on strengthening love and gratitude for yourself as a start.

"When you reinforce one strand at a time with love and gratitude, soon the whole web can withstand any perturbation that comes its way." (MFH)

Today's Prayer: *Spirit — who most needs my love, compassion, and kindness today?*

One thing I am grateful for this morning:

Today I Intend to:

Optional journaling exercise: Brainstorm ways that you can be more kind and compassionate to others, to build connections, or enhance communication. Then pick at least one person in your life to begin to put some of these ideas into practice.

> **Extra Credit:** Go back to the "Before You Begin" section (page 13) and reach out and connect with someone on your "People I love" list.

End Your Day

What I am grateful for today:

What didn't go so well today?

What did I learn from that?

Good stuff that happened:

How can I make tomorrow better?

(Day 33) Begin Your Day: _____

"No matter how much you might shut yourself off from Spirit, that loving, Divine energy is still with you, waiting for you to call upon it. Divine love is always there, ready to welcome you home when you gather up the courage to reach out.

"Sometimes that loving, Divine voice is quiet in your life, but 'quiet' doesn't mean 'gone.'" (AFTL, Chapter 14)

Today's Prayer: *I am ready and willing to see and experience Divine love in my life, and in the world around me.*

One thing I am grateful for this morning:

Today I intend to:

While you may at times feel disconnected from your Higher Power, I want you to know that **you cannot hide from Divine love.**

End Your Day

What I am grateful for today:

What didn't go so well today?

What did I learn from that?

Good stuff that happened:

How can I make tomorrow better?

(Day 34) Begin Your Day: _____

When I moved to Tacoma, Washington, I felt a bit lost and detached from my new neighbors. I had lived in Colorado for so long that I knew I needed a way to deeply connect with the folks around me. Then one day on a walk I saw it: a new community garden was under construction. I loved gardening but since had I moved into my new townhouse here, I no longer had room for my hobby. I viewed this garden project as the answer to my prayers for growing space. It turned out to be much more than just a plot of land on which to raise lettuce.

This garden was the brainchild of two engineers who worked for a local technology company. Their idea was to not only provide a space for company employees and the community to come together and bond over plants, but also to raise food to donate to local food banks.

When I joined, I pledged to donate at least half of my produce to local charities. That was not a problem as I could easily grow much more food than my family would eat anyway. But at the time I signed on, I didn't realize the benefits that I would receive back: bonds of friendship and connection with other people in the spirit of helping others. Growing food to give to those less fortunate helped me feel like I was contributing to the community in a very tangible way. Spending time with my fellow gardeners, people from all faiths, all backgrounds, and a diversity of ethnic heritages, gave me hope that humanity really can come together in peace and service. It also made me feel much more connected to my new town, and of course getting out of the house and digging in the dirt brought a sense of peace and calm to my day that is difficult for me to find anywhere else.

Our little community garden wasn't so small: over fifty families rented space to grow food and flowers. Some folks, like the founders, were the heart and soul of the place. For many other members, the garden was a spot to socialize, plan outings, and share tips on dealing with gardening challenges. For me, it warmed my heart to see so many diverse families coming together, forging connections to each other, and helping those less fortunate, with love and compassion.

Today's Prayer: *Spirit, in what ways can I help strengthen my connections to others around me?*

One thing I am grateful for this morning:

Make an effort to approach each person and each situation as a possibility to establish a positive connection.

End Your Day

What I am grateful for today:

What didn't go so well today?

What did I learn from that?

Good stuff that happened:

How can I make tomorrow better?

(Day 35) Begin Your Day: _____

Many people who have had mystical or spiritual experiences report hearing an unearthly music reverberating all around them. Experiencers often sense it not just with their ears, but also with their hearts. This music is haunting, inspiring, uplifting, and unforgettably beautiful. In fact it is so beautiful that after having heard it myself on several occasions, I have lost much of my desire to listen to human music.

This is the song of heaven, the music of the spiritual realm.

Heaven's song is the collective heart-voices of the angels, masters, and all other souls sending their love, gratitude, and joy back to Spirit. It is also the return energy of Divine love and connection echoing through the cosmos as a vibration that we sense as music.

But it isn't just spiritual beings in the afterlife who contribute to this song; each one of us here on Earth contributes to it, too. And that includes *you*.

You, just as you are right now with all of your talents, faults, joys, and sorrows, also contribute to that miraculous song of love and connection. Your love can add to its strength just as much as that of any angelic being. Every time you feel, act, or speak from a place of kindness, compassion, love, gratitude, appreciation, joy, enthusiasm, or even fun, you send out positive, spiritual energy. It radiates from you as a spiritual vibration, merging with the vibrations of love and gratitude from other beings, and becoming part of the harmony of the song of heaven.

So you see, the heavenly music doesn't just reside in the spiritual dimension, nor does it completely originate there. It actually *does* reverberate through our physical dimension so that our human bodies, in concert with our souls, can actually add to its harmony and depth. It is through this vibration or "music" that the Divine surrounds you in love and connects to you, even now, whether you can sense it or not.

I really do mean it when I say, "The love in your heart is Spirit's favorite song."

Today's Prayer: *Help me recognize and experience Divine love both in myself and in others.*

One thing I am grateful for this morning:

Today I Intend to:

When you see other people today, I want you to start considering how alike you are. **Focus on similarities rather than differences,** and know that others are a part of this Divine Universe, just like you.

End Your Day

What I am grateful for today:

What didn't go so well today?

What did I learn from that?

Good stuff that happened:

How can I make tomorrow better?

Extra Credit: Start your day off with a hug. Hug yourself, a loved one, or a pet. Hugs help us feel good, body, mind, and soul.

Week Five Review

Use these two pages to summarize your week. What did you experience or learn? Did you have any insights or aha moments? What went well? What would you like more of?

Sometimes a challenge is not a roadblock, but
is instead an opportunity to gain a new level of awareness.

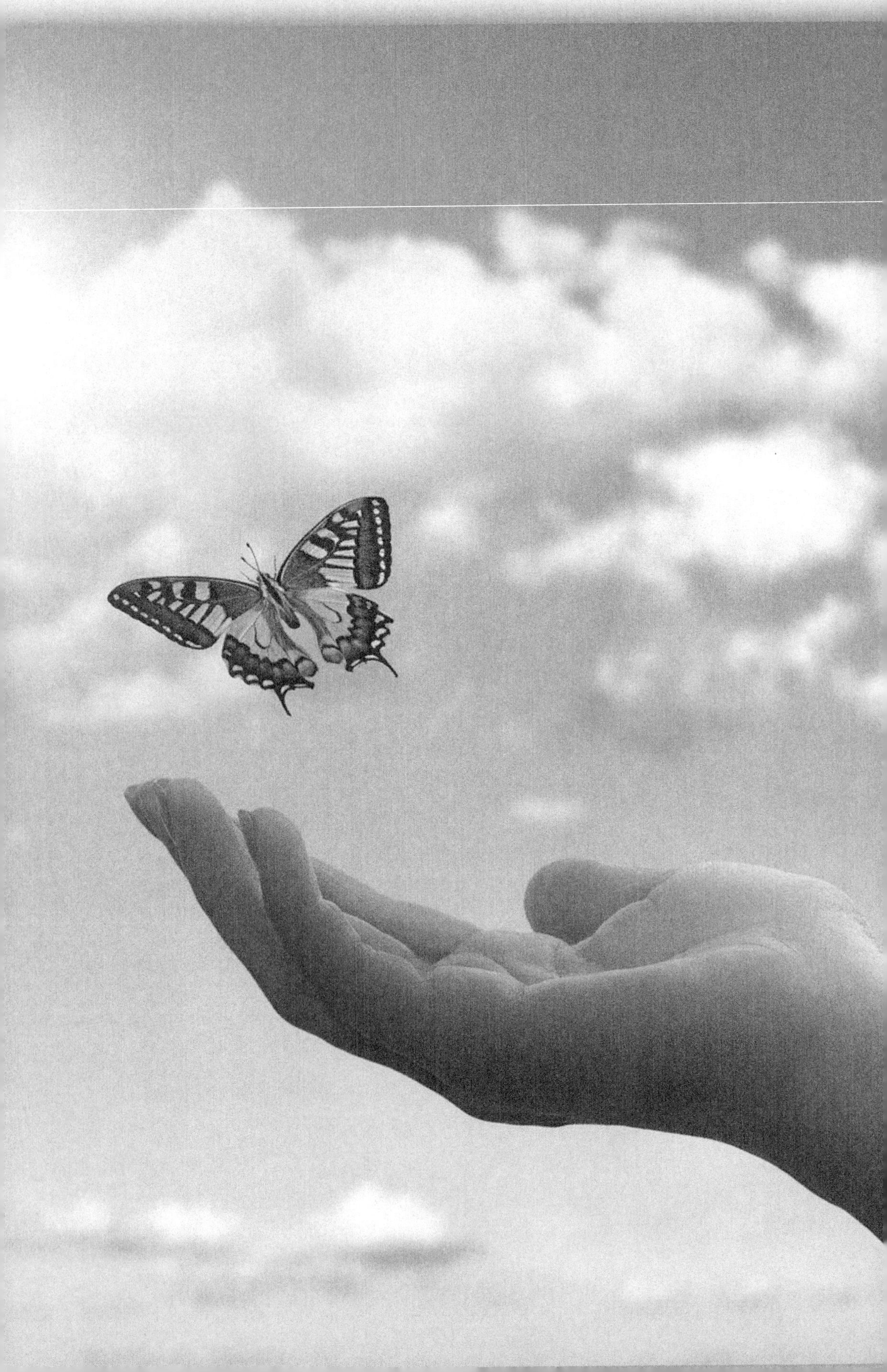

Week Six: Releasing and Allowing

Congratulations on reaching the halfway point! This week I will help you explore the importance of releasing things that keep you stuck, and challenge you to be open to letting go of beliefs and habits that are holding you back.

It's not unusual to carry around limiting memories, fears, thoughts, and beliefs; how you have been wronged, people who have wronged you, past traumas, anger, thoughts that you are not good enough, that being timid or small will keep you safe, and more. The origins of these beliefs vary from person to person, but I want to emphasize that you are not alone. Plenty of other people on this planet deal with the same things every day, and in my humble opinion it is these limiting beliefs that are not only keeping individuals stuck, but holding our society back as well.

In order to create a more expansive life, you have be willing to let go of your limiting beliefs. For me, it's usually best to do this gradually. I like to keep in mind the words of Rev. Martin Luther King, Jr., "Take the first step in faith. You don't have to see the whole staircase, just take the first step." This approach speaks to me not just of the first step on a staircase to ever-increasing awareness and love, but applies to every step of the journey including releasing those things that keep us stuck.

Let's look at this another way, through a story. One of the biggest hurdles that a beginning art student faces is letting go of preconceived ideas about the world around them. I am a great example of this. When I began taking art lessons, I would often paint shadows as jet black, grass as intense green, and clouds as pure white because that is how they were *supposed to be* in my mind. But when I stood back and looked at those early paintings I felt frustrated because they did not look *right* somehow. When my instructor would point out that I was trying to paint *what I thought I knew* about the subject, rather than what was *actually there*, I began to understand that my perception was clouded by what I believed to be true. I eventually learned how to really *see* without beliefs getting in the way, and how to let go of what I thought I knew. When I stopped seeing clouds as just white and recognized that they are most commonly shades of gray, blue, or purple, it was as if a new world opened to me. Sometimes clouds are red, orange, or golden, too. I needed to let go of those limiting beliefs before I could create an effective, beautiful painting that captured the essence of the scene before me.

Likewise, if you want to create a beautiful, fabulous life, it helps to release any attachments you have to fears, limitations, old thought patterns, ineffective ways of doing things, and any pre-judgments you might have. The first step in releasing anything is awareness, and that is the focus of this week.

(Remember that professional therapy is A-OK. Please seek out the assistance of a qualified therapist for help overcoming traumas, abuse, anger, rage, attention challenges, or anything else that seems too big to handle alone.)

(Day 36) Begin Your Day: _____

I didn't have a clue that my soul was working on yet another spiritual revelation when I was driving north out of Boulder, Colorado, one morning about a year and a half after my NDE. I thought about the past eighteen months and all I had worked through, including sadness and depression brought on by grief from missing my home in the afterlife. I pined for the spiritual realm: its peace, the enormity of Divine love, the easy connection to everyone and everything, the expansiveness, and the learning. Everyday life on Earth just seemed overly complicated and difficult in comparison. I knew that I should feel grateful for my life and my second chance, but deep down I experienced a vague sense of unease.

Writing my first book (*Awakenings from the Light*) helped me feel a little better because it gave me a sense of purpose, but it wasn't quite enough to help me achieve the state of internal peace that I desired. Even though I felt grateful for my life, and looked forward to the rest of it, I continued to battle those uneasy feelings. So every morning I began to ask Spirit to bring me clarity on why I was feeling this way.

Then came month eighteen, that morning I was driving from Boulder. No, it's not what you might think. I didn't crash and have another NDE. As my car descended that hill, a sudden realization came out of the blue: over the last eighteen months I had been carrying around a very quiet, deeply buried sense of anger that I was sent back here against my wishes.

Me, angry? That was not what I wanted to believe about myself, but yet there it was. Other people felt angry, not me. But it *was* me. And carrying those feelings around for so long caused that underlying sense of unease I felt for so long. A little ray of illumination began to shine on a shadow in my heart that lay hidden for months.

I wasn't nearly as grateful as I thought I was and realized just how much inner work I still had left.

When clarity came on that road north of Boulder, the residual anger about being sent back to life evaporated in a moment of pure love, understanding, and acceptance that seemed to come from outside of me. I pulled off the road at a safe place and simply let myself experience that grace, clarity, and love. I felt deeply apologetic about my prior anger while at the same time my gratitude for being here deepened and strengthened. I gently accepted that this was something I needed to learn, embrace with compassion and forgiveness, and let go of any sense of guilt or shame. My feeling of love for Spirit and for this life expanded beyond what had been possible for me just the day before. My heart opened up once again.

Today's Prayer: *Help me let go of one thing that is keeping my soul from soaring today.*

One thing I am grateful for this morning:

(We're taking a break from the normal evening questions in order to set up activities for the rest of this week.)

Things in my life that feel "stuck":

Practice for the week — The God Jar: Get a big, beautiful jar or vase that you don't use and clean it out. If you would like to bless it with a prayer, take time to do that now. This is now your "God Jar" (or call it "Spirit Jar" if you prefer). Prepare some small, blank pieces of paper or index cards. They don't need to be big — a few inches square will do. When you have a worry or a situation you need help with, write about it on the paper. Now fold up the paper, ask Spirit to handle it for you, and put it in the God Jar. Then simply go about your day. It will help you get the problem off your mind and put it on Spirit's list to handle. In time, when the God Jar gets full, you can bury the papers in your garden, safely burn them in a fireplace, or recycle them. See page 248 for more information.

(Day 37) Begin Your Day: _____

In order to truly transform yourself and your life, you must be willing to let go of the way things *used to be*. You *can* change — you have an innate capacity to choose and follow a new path. But open up your mind and heart to allow the old attachments, beliefs, and behaviors to fall away.

Today's Prayer: *Spirit, I desire clarity on the situation that is causing me the most stress.*

One thing I am grateful for this morning:

People I would like to forgive, and why:

Release what is stuck: Go back to yesterday morning's entry and pick one thing from your "things that feel stuck" list. Use this as your focus for the God Jar exercise today. See page 248 for more information on the God Jar.

End Your Day

What I am grateful for today:

What didn't go so well today?

What did I learn from that?

Good stuff that happened:

How can I make tomorrow better?

(Day 38) Begin Your Day: _____

"Experiencing an NDE can change the way someone views life. How could it not? Facing death, experiencing the 'afterlife', and then returning to Earth can change people. It changed me in one important way: it is a bit easier for me to let go of my need to control every little thing.

"I'm no longer terrified of death. Actually, I'm not scared of much of anything anymore. I suspect that because I died and had a glimpse of a grander, more conscious and connected reality, not much of this physical world frightens me. In that way, my NDEs have liberated me from the burden of the fears and worries I carried with me for most of my earlier life. It was those fears and worries that, I believe, drove me to want to control even the smallest aspect of my life." (AFTL, Chapter 11)

Today's Prayer: *Spirit, I am ready to release my fears and worries about _____. Please guide me in making this happen, for the good of all concerned.*

One thing I am grateful for this morning:

Fears that I am ready to release:

My suggestion for you today is to ask Spirit (aloud) for clarity on a particular situation that troubles you. Make sure you are sincere in the request, though. If you're not quite ready to face this situation, don't ask for clarity on it yet. When you have some quiet time, ask aloud something like this:

"Spirit, I desire clarity on _____. Show me what I need to know to make a loving decision and go forward in my life. Positive or negative, I can handle it. Please make it clear and obvious to me in the best timeframe for me. Thank you."

Then gently pay attention in your life for the answer. It will come, trust Spirit.

End Your Day

What I am grateful for today:

What didn't go so well today?

What did I learn from that?

Good stuff that happened:

How can I make tomorrow better?

(Day 39) Begin Your Day: _____

"Have you ever had the feeling that a part of your life was an uphill battle, that no matter how hard you tried, something wasn't going the way you planned? Roadblocks and obstacles kept popping up out of nowhere. Things happened that seemed to derail you from the path you were on. Yet you stubbornly continued on in the direction you laid out for yourself, hoping against hope that eventually it would all work out.

"Sometimes it does.

"But other times, struggling only digs the hole deeper beneath your feet. You might focus so much on the struggle itself that you don't see a slightly different path that will allow you to get what you really need or want. More importantly, your struggles and stubbornness may get in the way of spiritual grace working in your life.

"Let go. Give Spirit room to do some of the work. You don't have to control everything." (AFTL, Chapter 11)

Today's Prayer: *Today, I allow room for Divine grace to enter my life and lead me through my challenges to a place of peace and love.*

One thing I am grateful for this morning:

Beliefs about myself that I wish to release:

Contemplate: Is there a situation in your life where you are feeling out of control, or are trying to control too much? How have you dealt with this situation (or a similar one) in the past? Did that approach work? Is it working this time? How might you be able to change your thinking or actions to alter the energy of this situation and generate a different, more positive outcome?

Extra Credit: Go back to the "Before You Begin" section (page 13) and reach out and connect with someone on your "People I love" list.

End Your Day

What I am grateful for today:

What didn't go so well today?

What did I learn from that?

Good stuff that happened:

How can I make tomorrow better?

(Day 40) Begin Your Day: _____

A message from Nancy's spiritual guides:

Focus on making your *own life* beautiful. We have seen that the need to focus on others, and even control them, is yet another way that people like to distract themselves from taking a good look at their own lives and making positive changes. You might not want to face your inner self; the things you want to improve, the things that do not work so well, the truth of your life. So it is easy to distract yourself from your own self-work by focusing on on other people.

Are you open to releasing any need you might have to control others?

Are you willing to let go of what you think you know about other people, about life, and about yourself?

Are you willing to release your attachments to that which no longer works for you?

And most important of all, are you truly open and willing to embrace the magnificent being that you are right now?

Today's Prayer: *Divine Spirit, today I put my trust and faith in you.*

I desire clarity on releasing _____. Please make it clear and obvious to me whatever it is that I need to know or see to make a better way forward, for myself and the good of all concerned.

One thing I am grateful for this morning:

Anger I am carrying:

Contemplate: What other attachments do I have that may be keeping me stuck?

End Your Day

What I am grateful for today:

What didn't go so well today?

What did I learn from that?

Good stuff that happened:

How can I make tomorrow better?

Check In: How are you feeling, physically, emotionally, and spiritually?

(Day 41) Begin Your Day: _____

"As my Guide said in heaven said, the single toughest thing we humans can face is letting go of the need to be in complete control of everything — every person, situation, event, and environment — and allowing a little room for Spirit to work.

"The way she explained it to me is that in attempting to control everything, we effectively shut off our vision to many other good opportunities. We close the door to spiritual guidance with our need to control. Keeping the door open by letting go allows a little room for Spirit to work in our lives.

"There is also another important point to consider. Spiritual guidance often makes itself known to us in our quiet moments: when we're praying, meditating, walking in nature, riding in a car, sleeping, or other similar times. If we allow ourselves to have more of these quiet, unstructured moments, we can better hear that guidance coming through our inner knowing, our hearts, and that 'still, small voice' inside each of us.

"If you must structure your time, and most of us do to some extent, try to leave some quiet moments for yourself and God to commune. It might be that you choose to turn off your music during your commute, or schedule a 10-minute meditation into your day. You might choose to take a quiet walk during a break at work or spend some time in prayer at the end of the day. Any one of these things, if done consistently, can open you to Divine guidance." (AFTL, Chapter 11)

Today's Prayer: *Spirit, I ask for your assistance in helping me let go of the need to control _____ .*

One thing I am grateful for this morning:

The water exercise: Trying to control outside forces or other people is like trying to grasp water tightly in your hands. Go to a sink and turn on the water sometime today. Cup your hands together under the stream of water and hold as much in your hands as you can. Once your hands are filled with water, squeeze both hands into fists as if you were trying to grasp onto the water as tightly as possible. Go on, grab that water as hard as you can! What happens? The water is forced out of your hands and you completely lose the very thing you were trying to control. Life is often like this. The more you grasp at something, the more it can evade you.

Extra Credit: Use your morning lists from this week (fears, limiting beliefs, anger, etc.) in future exercises in letting go. Ask for help from the Divine in releasing those things that are holding you back by using the God Jar exercise (page 248). You do not need to do this alone.

End Your Day

What I am grateful for today:

What didn't go so well today?

What did I learn from that?

Good stuff that happened:

How can I make tomorrow better?

(Day 42) Begin Your Day: _____

One of the things I have worked on releasing recently is the idea of my daughter as a small child who still needed me. You might be able to relate to this if your children have grown and moved on with their lives. One of my friends admitted she had been a "hot mess" when her son made the transition from high school off to university. I didn't feel *that* impacted, just somewhat empty and wondering what I could do to feel as though I had a purpose again.

As my daughter graduated from high school and began to make her own decisions, like many parents I felt both elation and, yes, some concern. Had all of us in her family, including me, given her the skills she needed to be a happy, healthy adult? Would she make the best decisions for herself and her life? Would she ultimately be OK?

I relied on my connection to Spirit to get me through this challenging time and help me release any beliefs that held me back. This included learning how to embrace the idea of my daughter as an independent adult. Every morning I asked Spirit for guidance, love, and grace, and gradually my feelings shifted.

My daughter is now on her own, independent, and on her way to creating the life she desires. And I am looking forward to what lies ahead for both of us.

Today's Prayer: *Spirit, I ask for your guidance in becoming aware of the top things that are holding me back right now.*

One thing I am grateful for this morning:

Other things I wish to release:

Set aside some unstructured time today. I suggest aiming for 30 minutes. Avoid having a plan for this time. Simply set aside a part of your day to do something non-work related (and preferably non-electronic media) that is positive and helpful for you and anyone else you choose to include. When that time comes, go into your heart and mind and ask yourself what you *feel* that you want to do in that moment. Leave the "shoulds" out of it. What is the first thing that pops into your mind? Reading a novel? Going for a walk? Calling a friend? Spending time with you partner or kids? If it is a positive thing you have chosen, go ahead and do it.

End Your Day

What I am grateful for today:

What didn't go so well today?

What did I learn from that?

Good stuff that happened:

How can I make tomorrow better?

Week Six Review

Use these two pages to summarize your week. What did you experience or learn? Did you have any insights or aha moments? What went well? What would you like more of?

We are all connected to each other through Spirit.
What we wish for someone else, we are also wishing for ourselves.

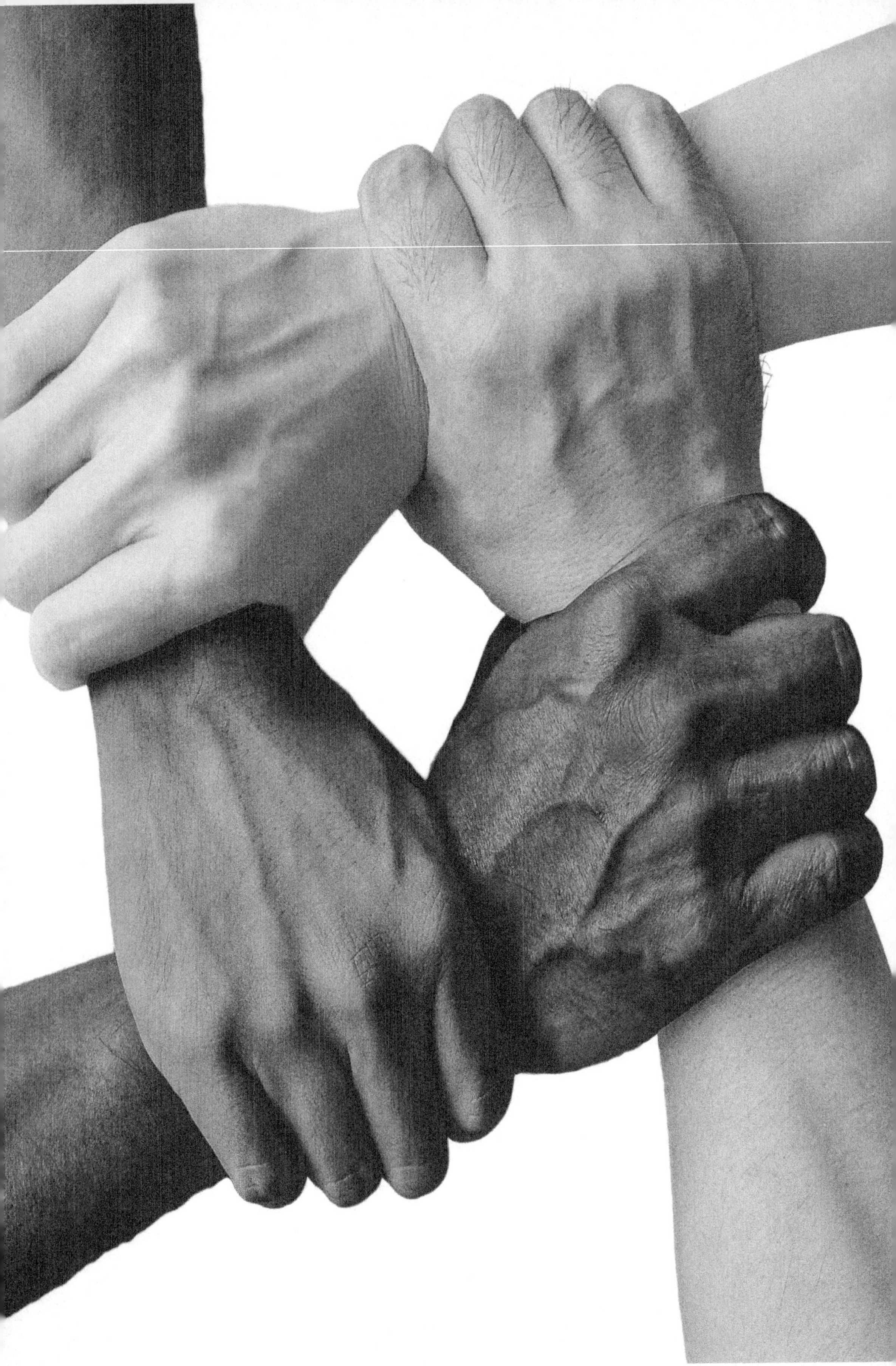

Week Seven: Building Community

Super job on making it to week seven! This week we will spend time considering the importance of belonging to, and creating, communities.

The summer of 2020 gave the entire world more awareness of just how important a sense of community is to both ourselves and societies. A global pandemic changed how we lived on a daily basis. In a short period of time, much of the world's population was asked to remain at home and avoid large, public gatherings. We were cut off from interacting in person with our familiar communities: schools, churches, neighborhood gatherings, clubs, and even extended families. Up until that point, a lot of us had taken the importance of these communities for granted. I know I did. I was used to being able to attend meetings, art shows, equestrian events, and hosting small dinner parties without giving it much thought. But now, doing these were completely off the table (at least for in-person events). For many, even our places of employment were suddenly off-limits, and isolation began to take its toll on our mental and physical health.

I hope the summer of 2020 will be a reminder for all of us just how important it is to stay connected with others, in person if possible.

This coming week I would love for you to give serious thought to the communities of which you are a part, and I do not simply mean the your town or neighborhood. If you do not have many connections with others, consider how you can forge new bonds. What communities can you join? How can you strengthen the bonds that you *do* have already?

Why is belonging to a community important? Turn the page to learn more.

(Day 43) Begin Your Day: _____

"Communities in the truest sense of the word are groupings of people with a common bond, coming together, and sharing *as one*. We might share a physical place, like a town, but we could also build a community around a shared goal or belief system. A community doesn't need to be a physical place — all it needs to flourish is a caring, sharing, like-minded group of people coming together for a common purpose. When we share with others by lending a hand, we build a network of support, of caring, and of love. In the most ideal communities, members enable each other to be their best. Allowing others to be giving and generous is one way to enable and encourage the best in each other and thus strengthen the community.

"My heavenly Guide wanted to inspire all of us to work more at building alliances of support, whether it's a community of friends, family, neighbors, church groups, or co-workers. She assured me that coming together in this way, in love and support of each other, would make a positive difference in everyone's lives." (AFTL, Chapter 12)

Today's Prayer: *Spirit, today I open my heart and allow myself to accept love, guidance, and support from you.*

One thing I am grateful for this morning:

Communities I belong to:

Practice for the week: Be of service to someone else each day this week, even in a small way. Respectfully helping others allows your love and kindness to transform your community.

End Your Day

What I am grateful for today:

What didn't go so well today?

What did I learn from that?

Good stuff that happened:

How can I make tomorrow better?

(Day 44) Begin Your Day: _____

"Demonstrate your love for others by giving them an opportunity to show love to you, and to live their lives authentically and with integrity.

"Allow others to help you when you need it, to be compassionate, make their own decisions and choices, and be responsible for their own lives. We are each on a different path. Love and respect the path each person is on, just as you would want them to love and respect yours." (AFTL, Chapter 12)

Today's Prayer: *Spirit, how can I best allow others to help me?*

One thing I am grateful for this morning:

Relationships I want to strengthen:

Allow others to show love and support to you today, even if it's in a small way. Leaving the space for others to be compassionate and giving, without your ego or fear getting in the way, is a supreme act of love and trust. If you are a very independent person, allowing others to help you may be one of the most challenging, but important, exercises of this entire program.

Extra Credit: Go back to the "Before You Begin" section (page 13) and review your "I Want to Learn" list. Choose one of them and take a step toward learning it. Locate a book, website, or class that will get you started.

End Your Day

What I am grateful for today:

What didn't go so well today?

What did I learn from that?

Good stuff that happened:

How can I make tomorrow better?

(Day 45) Begin Your Day: _____

Do you consider yourself an introvert, someone who is more energized by being alone or with very small groups of people? If you *are* more introverted, participating in large, noisy social events can feel exhausting. But even introverts need interaction with others and gain benefits from being part of a community, even if it is a small one. So how do you balance your preference for avoiding large gatherings with the benefits of belonging to a group of like-minded and like-hearted people?

As an introvert myself, I am (usually) happiest in small groups. I cultivate a few very close friendships, and typically feel uncomfortable at large, noisy events (especially parties). I prefer to find (or form) small groups to join: book clubs, outdoor activities clubs, art societies, spiritual discussion groups, photography clubs, and more. I also love to volunteer on local projects like trail maintenance, habitat restoration, or even fostering shelter dogs. Volunteer activities are often done with small groups of people and because we are all actively doing things, like rebuilding trails, rather than trying to make small talk, it is easier for people like me to feel comfortable and make a connection with someone else. When I *do* attend a group meeting, I devote time to learning about a few of my fellow attendees, and will get involved with the group as much as I can once I get to know its members.

Whether you are introverted, extroverted, or a mix of both, I encourage you to seek out and find at least one group to connect with this week. Remember, we all benefit from having community bonds.

Today's Prayer: *Allow me to see who needs my love and support today. And allow me to accept love and support from others.*

One thing I am grateful for this morning:

Today I Intend to:

Are you feeling isolated from those you love, cut off from your old support systems? Or have you recently moved to a new area and don't have many local friends? Today, take some time to brainstorm ways that you can begin to reach out to others, to join a community, or even create one.

End Your Day

What I am grateful for today:

What didn't go so well today?

What did I learn from that?

Good stuff that happened:

How can I make tomorrow better?

(Day 46) Begin Your Day: _____

"A part of our connection to others lies the ways that we come together to help each other. And just as we each have a desire to help others in need, others may want to help us when we need it. The kindest and most loving thing we can do is to let them. We can show our love or care to others by allowing them to show love, kindness, or compassion to us."

Many of us push others away when all they want is to lend a helping hand. Why? Pride, ego, the fear of being seen as "unable," maybe. Sometimes cultural norms tell us to be more independent as well. In some situations, it might be good for us to let go and allow others to step in and assist. It's OK if we are not strong and in control of everything all the time. Allowing space for others to be strong, to lend a hand, and to shine their light is a most loving and compassionate gesture.

Helping each other, and allowing others to shine too, starts the process of building a community around us, in Spirit. (AFTL, Chapter 12)

Today's Prayer: *Spirit, help us all strengthen our connections to each other on this planet. And help me strengthen my connection to _____ today.*

One thing I am grateful for this morning:

Communities I want to join (or create):

Contemplate some ways you can help others. Can you assist an elderly neighbor to shovel her sidewalk clear of snow? Do you have an ailing family member who needs to travel to the grocery store or pharmacy? How about paying the fee for the person behind you at the toll booth or the entrance to the national park you're visiting? Jot down ways that you could help others, here:

End Your Day

What I am grateful for today:

What didn't go so well today?

What did I learn from that?

Good stuff that happened:

How can I make tomorrow better?

Extra Credit: Go back to the "Before You Begin" section (page 13) and reach out and connect with someone on your "People I love" list.

(Day 47) Begin Your Day: _____

"Many of us have moved away from having a sense of community in our busy, modern lives. We've isolated ourselves by choice or necessity. The electronic age can make it difficult to build true, in-person, meaningful friendships. We get caught up in online games, social media, and texting, forgetting that the real connections come when we're face-to-face. I think we've also lost something else truly valuable and sacred: that sense of an almost tribal community that, in some ways, is so integral to being human.

"For most of our time on Earth as a species, humans tended to live in small, close-knit communities or tribal groups. At the most basic level, these small groups helped us survive and thrive. Today we live in large cities surrounded by millions of people, yet rarely speak to our neighbors and don't connect with co-workers any more than we have to. But that mental and emotional need to be part of a community is still ingrained in our psyches, perhaps even in our DNA.

"Opening up some space in our independence, allowing others to help us, and in turn lending a hand to others is how we can start to form or strengthen a small community of support. I've seen this work within my own life. My trauma and recovery has been a blessing in a way. I've come to see the value in relaxing those defenses and letting others in. I understand now that I'm not a superwoman, I do need and want help sometimes. I've noticed that this softening of my walls of independence has helped me more easily build new relationships and strengthen existing friendships. Amazing what a little "allowing" can do!" (AFTL, Chapter 12)

Today's Prayer: *Spirit, I thank you for helping me to open up the space in my life to let others in.*

One thing I am grateful for this morning:

Today I Intend to:

Do you have comfort zones when it comes to reaching out to others or belonging to communities? List out what is comfortable for you and what is not. What step could you take to expand your comfort zones? Would you be willing to take that step this week?

End Your Day

What I am grateful for today:

What didn't go so well today?

What did I learn from that?

Good stuff that happened:

How can I make tomorrow better?

(Day 48) Begin Your Day: _____

Love starts now.
It starts with me.

I take responsibility.
I will change my life, with love.
I will help change my community, with love.
I will help change my nation, through love.
I will help change my planet, through love.

Love starts now.
Love starts with me.

One thing I am grateful for this morning:

Today I Intend to reach out to others by:

💡 Know that you ARE love, and you are a part of this amazing, Divine universe!

Extra Credit: What community would you like to join or create? Think about one step could you take today toward joining or forming that community. Then take that one step in the next week.

End Your Day

What I am grateful for today:

What didn't go so well today?

What did I learn from that?

Good stuff that happened:

How can I make tomorrow better?

(Day 49) Begin Your Day: _____

"At the time of my accident and NDE in 2014, most of my adult family lived out of state. I had one niece about an hour away from my home, but my siblings were scattered across the USA. Consequently, the first people to come to support me in the hospital were friends and coworkers who lived close by. Their presence so quickly after my accident let me know that I wasn't alone, that I was cared for, and that I had people who would be there to help me through what lay ahead. Having people come to hold my hand helped me feel that I was truly supported, and was not alone. Even though my body hurt, my heart felt warm and glowing from their presence.

"When I was struck by the SUV, I had been working at a small software company in Boulder, Colorado. For those who don't know Boulder, it has a reputation for being a mecca of elite professional and amateur athletes. Cyclists, rock climbers, trail runners, mountaineers, and adventure athletes of all kinds seem to make up 80% of the population. Scientists or software engineers by day turn into serious athletic warriors after 5 PM. My coworkers were no exception. When they heard the news that I'd been struck by a vehicle while riding my bicycle, they couldn't step in fast enough to help. Not only was I a coworker, I was a member of the local cycling community. The accident could have happened to any one of them. Not only did several of them visit me in the hospital, they helped me as I recuperated at home too. Once I came home they delivered food and meals to me for six weeks, helped out around my home, bought and delivered little things that I needed to make life easier, donated vacation time to me, and most importantly, worked at keeping my spirits up.

"This community support was something I really didn't expect and because of that, their generosity brought tears to my eyes many times. While I liked my coworkers and enjoyed being in the office, only a very few of them had become close friends. But almost everyone helped out in one way or another — even those I had rarely worked with and barely knew. The outpouring of support from this very unexpected community still chokes me up today." (AFTL, Chapter 14)

Today's Prayer: *Spirit, please assist me to see how I can assist others while also respecting their own paths through life.*

One thing I am grateful for this morning:

Think about your life over the last few weeks. Has someone offered to lend a hand in a healthy, supportive, caring way? Did you accept the help or not? If not, why not? If you did accept the help, how did it make you feel? How do you think it made the other person feel?

End Your Day

What I am grateful for today:

What didn't go so well today?

What did I learn from that?

Good stuff that happened:

How can I make tomorrow better?

Week Seven Review

Use these two pages to summarize your week. What did you experience or learn? Did you have any insights or aha moments? What went well? What would you like more of?

Love is the key to opening up the doorway
to the depths of your soul, your connections to others, and to
the higher realms of Spirit.

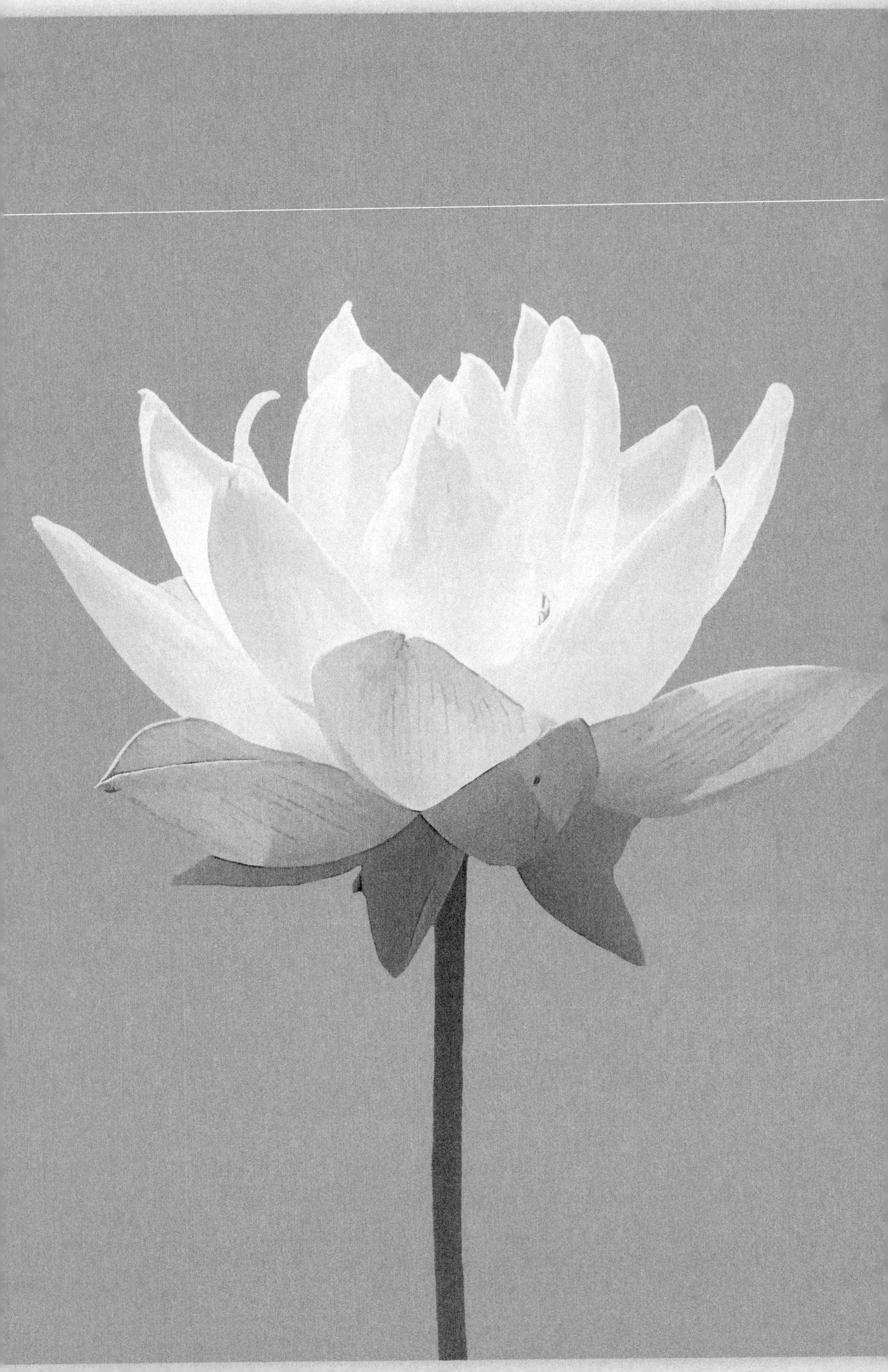

Week Eight: Your Intuition

I hope that this coming week of exploring your intuition will be fun, full of insights, and give you ideas to try for yourself. At the very least, I would love for you to come away with a renewed sense of connection to Spirit and ways to help you grow your heart-centered connection to Divine wisdom.

Let's start with a seemingly simple question: what is intuition?

For me, it is that sense of knowing something without going through a long, drawn-out, analytical thought process. It is often a felt-sense of simply *understanding* the right decision to make, answer to a question, or even what the best route home from work is (without consulting an app on your phone).

I also call this intuitive sense my *heart-voice*, since for me it seems to originate from that loving, spiritual center around my heart.

But what is it, really? I delve more into this question in *Awakenings from the Light*, but in short, I see it as the voice of Divine wisdom making itself known. It is more than the combination of personal experience, book-learning, or analytical thought processes. Intuition may be guidance from Spirit, a nudge from a spiritual guide, or even more rarely a deceased loved one. It could also be the voice of our own souls, and perhaps all of these things at once.

I have found that the best way to cultivate intuition for myself is to:

1) Align with the highest Divine guidance every morning
2) Make quiet time every day
3) Ask questions of Spirit
4) Be open for answers
5) Listen more, and maintain curiosity

This week is just a small sampling of ideas and techniques for increasing intuition in your life. For more ideas, check out my book, *Awakenings from the Light*, or read *Divine Intuition* by Lynn Robinson.

(Day 50) Begin Your Day: _____

"Even while on Earth we have direct access to Divine guidance. It may not always be easy for us to hear, but it is there if we know where to look. This guidance is what we call our inner wisdom, that internal sense of *just knowing*. It's what can help lead us in our choice of career, spouse, home, route home from work, or even vacation destination.

"This inner wisdom might also tell us when a family member is hurting, even though we're far apart. It can guide us in small decisions — whether to date someone or walk away, whether a place of worship is right for us, or whether that nagging pain in our side is something serious.

"Our inner wisdom is a combination of our intuition or "gut-sense," our heart-voice, and our mind or learned knowledge. When accessed in concert, they can be powerful resources for us to call on when making decisions.

"Intuition is that sense of coming to a conclusion quickly, getting a flash of insight, or making a fast decision independent of long, thought-filled reasoning or logic.

"Our heart-voice is that emotional, feeling-sense that we might have when making a decision or meeting someone. It's our spiritual compass, a direct link to our spiritual Source and spiritual wisdom.

"Our mind is a collection of our processed experiences combined with what we've learned either through formal channels, our families, or through life's hard knocks. The mind can be particularly susceptible to unfounded fears, pathologies, the effects of poor nutrition or health, or even brainwashing or propaganda.

"Even with practice, it still might be challenging to hear spiritual guidance over the chatter of your own mind. Practice stilling your mind too, in addition to your speech and hearing. Sometimes this quiet mind can happen spontaneously while you're doing something else: walking, sitting by a lake, riding on a train, or working on a craft." (AFTL, Chapter 13)

Today's Prayer: *Spirit, how can I better access your guidance?*

One thing I am grateful for this morning:

Practice for the week: Start experimenting with the three-part check when you are confronted with a decision. Begin small, with decisions that are not going to significantly impact yourself or others. 1) What does your intuition or gut say to do? 2) What do your emotions tell you? 3) And what does your mind think about this? Do they all agree? If not, why not?

End Your Day

What I am grateful for today:

What didn't go so well today?

What did I learn from that?

Good stuff that happened:

How can I make tomorrow better?

(Day 51) Begin Your Day: _____

How can you begin to further develop and trust your intuition? I started by having fun with it.

When I lived near Tacoma, Washington, I liked to experiment with my intuition when it was time to hop in the car and run errands. Traffic in that area could more closely resemble a parking lot at times rather than a roadway. Even worse, the bottlenecks could be unpredictable in both location and timing, so a traffic app was a necessity.

I decided to build and test my intuition by refusing to use my traffic app when running errands. Taking some deep breaths and gently quieting my mind before leaving home, I would *feel* the direction my inner knowing wanted me to take. Once at my destination, I would check the traffic app to see if my intuition had been correct. Had other routes been slower than the one my intuition chose? About 85 to 90% of the time, my intuition was correct.

Many times my inner sense would tell me to take a bizarre, unexpected route, and in all of *these* instances, it was also correct. The causes of the traffic jams in these cases were typically large accidents in unusual locations; in other words, places that normally were safe experienced an unusual accident or similar event. Once it was a water main that had just burst. Another time it was a disabled train blocking a crossing. All were things my mind did not know when I set off on my drive.

I then wondered what would happen if I ignored my intuition and followed that voice in my brain, to take the route experience told me that I *should* take. Almost every time I ignored my intuition and followed the voice of reason I ran into traffic jams, and one day it was a backup that lasted 90 minutes in a location that normally never saw traffic issues.

If you want to explore and expand your intuitive sense, try to figure out ways that you safely and easily test it, like I did with running errands.

Today's Prayer: *Guide me to the path that is for my best and highest good today.*

One thing I am grateful for this morning:

Cultivate quiet time at home this week: I have noticed that my inner voice is enhanced when I make my home a quiet zone. I turn off all noise-making media and simply let my mind and muse wander in that stillness. I realize this may not be easy for you, please try it. The constant media assault on our senses dampens our unique inner voices, our creativity, and can increase stress levels which further drowns out that inner wisdom.

End Your Day

What I am grateful for today:

What didn't go so well today?

What did I learn from that?

Good stuff that happened:

How can I make tomorrow better?

(Day 52) Begin Your Day: _____

If Spirit could speak to you now, It might say this:

I speak to you on the winds,
With the surf,
With a laugh,
And with a cry.
My call to you lies in the recesses of your being,
Deep in your heart.
Heed that call to hear me in your life.

Let your heart-voice guide you.
What does it whisper?
To love more?
To help a stranger?
To be your true self?

Today's Prayer: *Spirit, I desire to heal any challenges or blocks in my connection to you. Please guide me to the best way to do this, for my highest good.*

One thing I am grateful for this morning:

Today I Intend to:

Challenge: Have you had times or experiences where the world has seemed to fade away and all of your being is enraptured by the task at hand? What were you doing when this happened? Try recreating it sometime this week.

End Your Day

What I am grateful for today:

What didn't go so well today?

What did I learn from that?

Good stuff that happened:

How can I make tomorrow better?

Extra Credit: Go back to the "Before You Begin" section on page 12 and review your "Inspires/Energizes Me" list. Choose one topic or activity to incorporate into your week.

(Day 53) Begin Your Day: _____

"Many of us are bound up in fears, and fears will drown out our inner wisdom quicker and more thoroughly than anything else. Fear is the opposite of love. Fear is often not our friend, especially unfounded fear (i.e., fear without a concrete reason). For example, being fearful of someone who is intending to hurt us is justified and helpful, but being generally fearful without a direct reason or cause can harm us. This type of fear stresses our bodies and minds, causes anxiety, and makes that inner, spiritual guidance more difficult to observe.

"It might help to ask yourself and your inner wisdom if there is truth in the fear. Is there something you can learn from it? Is there something you need to pay attention to? Does this situation or person remind you of something else that caused you harm? Our subconscious minds can often see trouble where our conscious minds don't. The subconscious can alerts us to potential trouble though fear. For example, a woman who was abused as a child might feel an instant fear of a new acquaintance who happens to remind her of her abuser.

"Think about the fear — is it trying to tell you something about a person or an event that your conscious mind can't see? If the fear doesn't seem to have an apparent cause, sometimes thinking through it helps to dispel it. Mull over what could *really* happen in the situation that you fear, whether a dire result is truly likely, and what the other, more positive, results might be. Bring a little logic to the situation if you can." (AFTL, Chapter 13)

Today's Prayer: *I am feeling fear about _____. What do I need to know about this fear in order to release it, and how can I work through it for my best and highest good?*

One thing I am grateful for this morning:

Today I Intend to:

Know that you are a strong, beautiful, courageous being of love and light, today and every day.

End Your Day

What I am grateful for today:

What didn't go so well today?

What did I learn from that?

Good stuff that happened:

How can I make tomorrow better?

Extra Credit: Lynn Robinson's book *Divine Intuition*, is an excellent resource if you would like more information on increasing your intuitive abilities.

(Day 54) Begin Your Day: _____

"Five months after my accident, I made a pledge to live a year listening to, and following, the voices of my heart and intuition rather than blindly doing only what my brain told me I should do. I knew from experience that following only the voice of knowledge in my mind didn't often bring me happiness or put me on a good, healthy path. In fact, that voice of knowledge often led me down roads that I wish now I had not taken, or asked me to close doors that in hindsight I would have been better off walking though.

"I prefer to call the combination of heart-voice, intuition, and mind my inner wisdom. I see them as distinct voices that give slightly different viewpoints on a person, situation, or decision. To me, in the best circumstances, they all work together in balance and harmony. At least they should, in theory. Some of us, though, have learned to listen to one of these three and ignore the other two. This was me: for years, I listened only to the voice of my mind and ignored my heart and intuition.

"Listening to my intuition and heart is a different approach to living than I have allowed myself in the past. While I haven't abandoned logic or reasoning, I do make a real effort to put much more weight on the guidance of my heart and intuition now." (AFTL, Chapter 13)

Today's Prayer: *Spirit, I love and appreciate your presence in my life. How can I best be of service to You?*

One thing I am grateful for this morning:

Today my heart wants:

Optional journaling exercise: Have your heart and intuition been trying to tell you something important or lead you down a different path in life? Sometimes this shows up as a sense of unease or low-level anxiety. Other times you might feel that something isn't quite right. Jot down what you have been feeling or hearing from your inner wisdom. Have you followed this wisdom yet, or even thought about following it? Why or why not? Is anything preventing you from following this path? Make sure to list out any fears or objections you might have, and then consider where they might be originating. Are these fears or objections valid right now? Can you work through them, or do you even want to work through them?

End Your Day

What I am grateful for today:

What didn't go so well today?

What did I learn from that?

Good stuff that happened:

How can I make tomorrow better?

(Day 55) Begin Your Day: _____

"If I have an opportunity put in front of me, I think about whether it feels 'right' for me to pursue it. I do a gut-check, a heart-check, and a mind-check. Do they all agree? If not, why? What is each voice of wisdom trying to tell me?

"The best scenario is if all three voices agree on the path ahead. If one doesn't agree, I spend time in contemplation. Am I feeling unfounded fear? Is there something about the situation to which I need to pay attention? Why are my intuition, heart, and mind telling me different things?

"If it does *feel* right and no one is going to get suffer as a result, I do it.

"One other benefit of living more from my heart and intuition is that my artistic creativity and productivity have skyrocketed. I can't wait to get to the easel every day, ideas flow effortlessly (so many that I can't keep up), and my craft of painting is better than it's ever been. Many more opportunities related to my art are flowing to me easily and more quickly than I ever would have imagined, perhaps because I am living more in alignment with who I am meant to be.

"And overall, I notice that I am more open, more buoyant, and, well, just plain happier. What's not to like about that?" (AFTL, Chapter 13)

Today's Prayer: *Thank you for leading me to boundless opportunity by listening to the voice of my heart.*

One thing I am grateful for this morning:

Today I Intend to cultivate quiet time by:

Today, simply **pay attention to any wisdom** you receive from your heart-voice or your intuition, especially during or after your quiet time. Jot it down here:

End Your Day

What I am grateful for today:

What didn't go so well today?

What did I learn from that?

Good stuff that happened:

How can I make tomorrow better?

(Day 56) Begin Your Day: _____

"During my NDE, my Guide taught me that one of the most important things we can do for ourselves is to learn how to access our own inner wisdom. To make it easier, try to cultivate a quiet mind. You can begin to quiet your mind through prayer, meditation, contemplation, playing a musical instrument, going for a hike without any music or noisy cell phones, wandering through a meadow or forest, or even sitting and enjoying a place that is sacred or special in some way. If you remove yourself from the distractions of modern life for a little bit each day, you can more easily learn to reconnect with your Divine Source." (AFTL, Chapter 13)

Today's Prayer: *Spirit, today I am open to receiving guidance that will help me expand my comfort zones to more clearly hear your guidance.*

One thing I am grateful for this morning:

Are you afraid of your intuition? Why or why not?

If you haven't already, **start experimenting with your intuition.** Pay attention when you get a strong knowing or feeling (not a thought, but a knowing or feeling). An example might be getting a strong feeling to take a different way home from work one day. If following this feeling won't hurt anyone or impact you too much, try listening to it. What happens? Was your feeling correct?

Extra Credit: Have you had intuitive experiences that have been particularly strong? Journal about them and look for common threads that could help you live from a more intuitive space.

End Your Day

What I am grateful for today:

What didn't go so well today?

What did I learn from that?

Good stuff that happened:

How can I make tomorrow better?

Week Eight Review

Use these two pages to summarize your week. What did you experience or learn? Did you have any insights or aha moments? What went well? What would you like more of?

Check In: How are you feeling, physically, emotionally, and spiritually?

If you make all of your decisions from
a place of fear,
You will never experience true freedom.

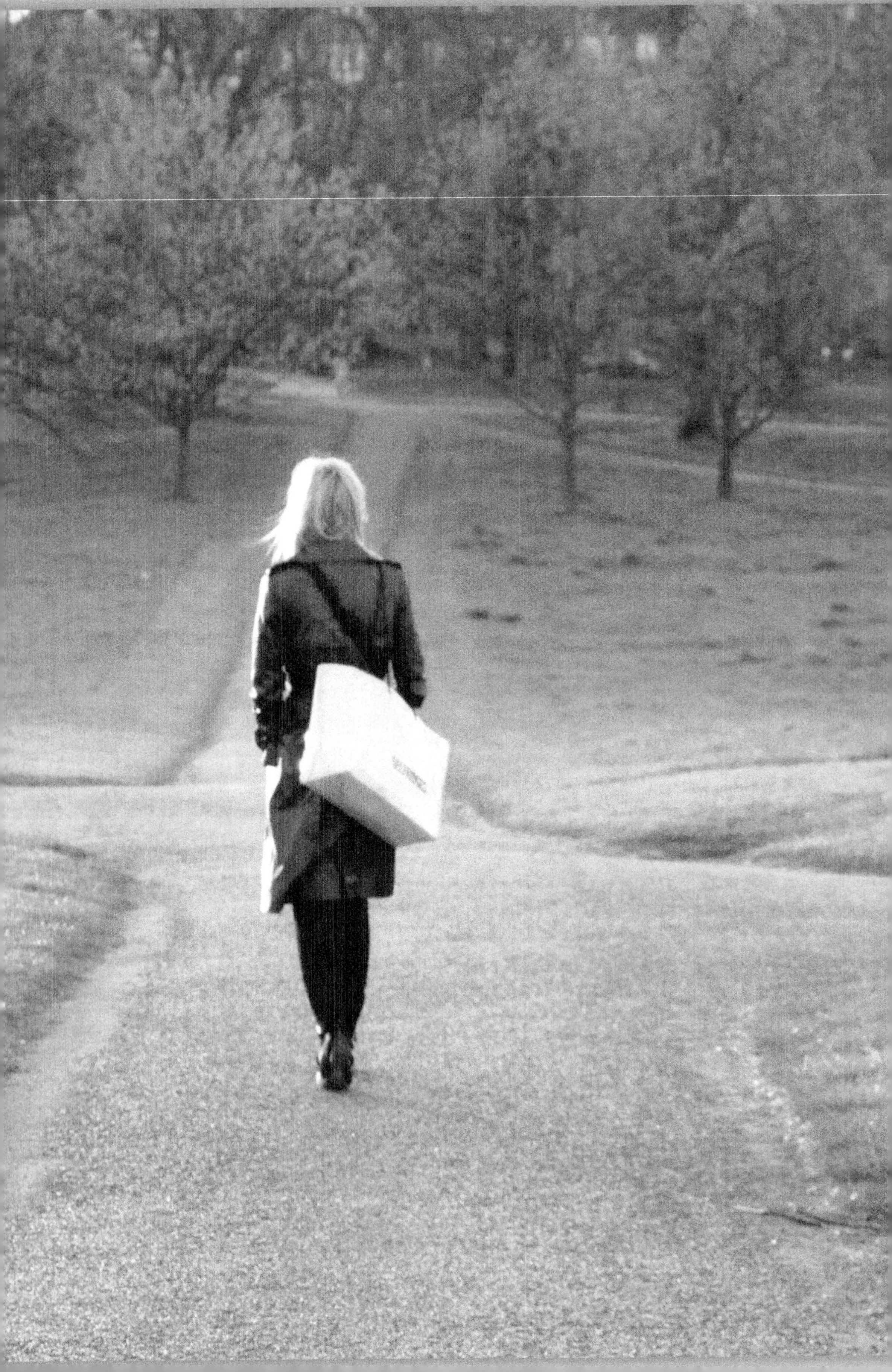

Week Nine: Choice

Congratulations, you are now on week nine and in the homestretch of this book.

This week is dedicated to the choices you make every day, and exploring the power you have in your ability to choose.

Whether you consciously realize it or not, each day you make countless choices or decisions, then take actions based on those choices. But are these decisions most often made from a higher state of awareness (i.e., love, compassion, kindness, or peace) or from a lower state such as fear or anger? All your work so far in this program contributes to your ability to make choices more consistently from a place of awareness and strength, but this week we will delve into this topic a little more deeply.

One of the events commonly reported among near-death experiencers (NDErs) is what is termed a "life review." This is an exercise the soul goes through after it leaves the physical body in which it is shown its decisions and actions made during the course of its lifetime. The soul is also shown, and often allowed to experience firsthand, the impact those choices made on everyone else. A life review is not meant to be a punishment. Instead, it is a tool for reflection and awareness ultimately resulting in learning and growth for the soul.

My own life review opened my eyes to the depths of connection we have to each other. It also helped me develop more compassion for myself and those around me, as well as become more consciously aware of how my decisions and actions affect other people.

While I cannot give you a real life review[6] to help you understand the impacts of your decisions or increase your capacity for love, I will help you begin to explore how your choices and actions can impact yourself and others.

---

[6] For more information, read *10 Life-Changing Lessons from Heaven* by Jeff Janssen.

(Day 57) Begin Your Day: _____

Ultimately, our most powerful tool for this life is the power of choice over our thoughts, words, and actions. Used wisely and with compassion, choice is our most incredible gift and tool for living the lives we want.

"One of the strongest visuals my Guide gave me during my time in heaven centered around the power that we have in the choices we make. It came as we walked along a creek in a little valley that wound among some ancient-looking, worn-down mountains. I gazed at the mountains and trees, enjoying the peaceful scene. Then we happened upon a small pond. Its water was dark and deep, and a few colorful leaves floated on its surface. My Guide instructed me to kneel by the water's edge. When I did, I sensed this wasn't an ordinary pond. She asked me to gently touch the surface to see what happened. Well, it was a pond, I knew what would happen but I followed her instruction anyway. By now I knew to simply do as I was told.

"Ripples emanated outward from the place I touched the water. The leaves moved up and down in response to the ripples that moved under them. But superimposed on the ripples I saw the choices that I'd made in my life. Those choices, like the ripples, made little waves in the world around me. They affected other people. They affected my future. And they somehow affected my past, too. Good or bad, my choices had an impact." (AFTL, Chapter 15)

Today's Prayer: *Spirit, today I desire your help in seeing the outcomes of my choices more clearly.*

One thing I am grateful for this morning:

Today I Intend to:

Practice: Before you make any important decisions this week, take some time to consider your choices. Are you approaching this decision from a place of love, compassion, kindness, or strength? Or are you fearful, angry, or uncertain of something? If the latter, consider how you can bring one or more of those higher levels of awareness into making the decision.

Extra Credit: Go back to the "Before You Begin" section (page 13) and review your "I Want to Learn" list. Choose one of them and take a step toward learning it. Locate a book, website, or class that will get you started.

End Your Day

What I am grateful for today:

What didn't go so well today?

What did I learn from that?

Good stuff that happened:

How can I make tomorrow better?

(Day 58) Begin Your Day: _____

A message from Nancy's spiritual guides:

You are beloved of the Divine. Your soul exists in light and beauty. We would like you to know that in your human life, you can live more from this state as well. It is ultimately your choice in how you live, but we think it would be a blissful experience if more people were to choose love and peace even just a little more than they are doing now.

You choose love and peace in following the path of your heart, the path of the Divine. When you need to make a decision, choose the one that will result in the most love for all. That necessitates getting in touch with your higher guidance through the path of your heart. Feel out the path of your life with the wisdom inherent in your soul.

The love and peace you cultivate will be a beacon for others, too. When you choose to live more from love, your spiritual essence will glow with an energy like no other. You can mentor others in this path of love simply by living it.

Love is your link to the Divine. And your choosing to build and strengthen love in your life helps bolster the entire field of Divine love.

Today's Prayer: *Spirit, today I walk in your love and light. All I do and say is from love and light.*

One thing I am grateful for this morning:

Today I Intend to:

Journal about a time when you have either intentionally or unintentionally harmed someone else. How might the other person have viewed you after this incident? How do you think the other person might have felt? What amends can you make, if any? What can you learn from this in order to make better choices in the future? Then journal about a time when you helped someone else. How do you think the other person might have felt? How did helping someone else make you feel?

End Your Day

What I am grateful for today:

What didn't go so well today?

What did I learn from that?

Good stuff that happened:

How can I make tomorrow better?

(Day 59) Begin Your Day: _____

"Think about what you can do to align your thoughts, feelings, words, and actions with what you desire to bring into your life.

"From a more spiritual viewpoint, the concept of 'manifesting' deals with energy. The realm of Spirit is, at its core, energetic. Its structure is the energy of love. Divine love permeates and forms the structure of everything. *Everything.* There is nowhere that love is not. I saw and experienced this quite vividly while I was near death.

"Let that sink in for a moment: *there is nowhere that love is not.*

"Here's the kicker: *the core or structure of our physical world is also the energy of spiritual love.* Our physical realm contains a loving energy at its core. Love helps to form the structure of our world just as love forms the structure of the spiritual realm. We have the added layer of 'physical-ness' here, but at its core, everything contains the energy of love.

"Since our thoughts, feelings, words, and actions emanate from us as energy, they can positively or negatively impact the loving energy that forms the world around us too, just like the ripples on the pond affect a leaf floating on its surface." (AFTL, Chapter 15)

Today's Prayer: *I desire the strength, courage, and patience to make thoughtful, powerful choices today and every day.*

One thing I am grateful for this morning:

Today I Intend to own my power by taking responsibility for my decisions and actions.

Interested in reading more about the concepts of intention and manifesting from a real rocket scientist? Add ***The Science Behind the Secret*** by Dr. Travis Taylor to your reading list. Dr. Taylor presents compelling reasons why it is important to approach decisions from a state of awareness and love.

End Your Day

What I am grateful for today:

What didn't go so well today?

What did I learn from that?

Good stuff that happened:

How can I make tomorrow better?

(Day 60) Begin Your Day: _____

A message from Nancy's spiritual guides:

Why bother choosing to walk the path of light and love in this seemingly mundane, sometimes harsh world? Why try to grow spiritually? What will it do for you?

    Choosing this path will help you blossom into the understanding that Divine, universal love and grace are for you too, in your life right now as well as in heaven. Taking steps toward this understanding opens you up to yet more grace. You might not feel worthy of it, or have done things in your past for which you have not forgiven yourself. Perhaps you think you are not good enough to receive that amount of unconditional love and support, or that that your previous actions are insurmountable.

    In this moment, open yourself up to the idea, the glimmer of a hope, that you are better than your past, that your mistakes are not the shackles you believe them to be. Be open to the idea that you can release them, and thus take steps to living in true freedom.

    You *are* worthy, right here and now.

Today's Prayer: *Spirit, how can I be more open to Your grace and love?*

One thing I am grateful for this morning:

A challenging decision I made, how I handled it, and how it turned out:

Practice: Make a choice to live from an active space of gratitude and grace this week. Say thank you as often as you feel gratitude during the day. At the end of the day, write down or recite aloud at least three things for which you are grateful. Also think about all of the good that happens today, and ponder what you can learn from the not-so-good things that came into your life so that you can make better choices in the future.

End Your Day

What I am grateful for today:

What didn't go so well today?

What did I learn from that?

Good stuff that happened:

How can I make tomorrow better?

(Day 61) Begin Your Day: _____

"Our thoughts, words, feelings, and actions travel out from us as ripples on a pond travel outward from the drop of a pebble on its surface. It doesn't matter whether our thoughts, words, feelings, and actions are positive or negative, they still travel outward from us. If a leaf is floating on the surface of that pond, it will move in response to the energy of the ripple that passes under it. It's all energy, radiating out from its source and interacting with all it contacts.

"Our words and actions affect others and the world around us, just as those ripples moved the leaf on the surface of the pond. Choosing to act in positive ways, and thus sending out high-vibrational thoughts, words, feelings, and actions changes the energy around us, which can then pass on to others. That positivity can uplift and encourage others, as well as ourselves." (AFTL, Chapter 15)

Today's Prayer: *How can I bring more of your love and light in this world?*

One thing I am grateful for this morning:

Today I Intend to:

Realize that living more intentionally and mindfully is a journey rather than a destination. No one expects you to be perfect. Simply make a conscious effort to do the best you can to be more present, centered, peaceful, or loving today.

Extra Credit: Watch a video that shows ripples from a rainstorm hitting the surface of a pond, or a pebble being dropped on its surface. Alternatively, if you can actually (and safely) visit a real pond, touch its surface and watch the ripples that you produce. Then think about your own life and choices, and how your decisions have traveled outward from you just like those ripples on the surface of the pond.

End Your Day

What I am grateful for today:

What didn't go so well today?

What did I learn from that?

Good stuff that happened:

How can I make tomorrow better?

(Day 62) Begin Your Day: _____

It was six days after the bicycling accident that put me in the hospital, and three days after my surgery and NDE. I woke very early that morning to the beautiful golden light just beginning to brighten my hospital room. I laid there, trying my best to feel grateful for simply being alive when a wave of self-pity and outrage washed through my mind. Why had this happened to me? Would the woman who hit me change her life, or even get real justice? How in the world would I be able to come out of this OK?

In those moments, I had serious doubts that my life would ever be normal again despite what my spiritual Guide told me during my NDE. And I conveniently did not want to remember that this whole event was part of my life plan to begin with.

Between hours of feeling deep gratitude and seeing love all around me, I'd have those fear-filled moments when my ego wanted to bask in its victimhood. This feeling of victimhood, coupled with sheer panic at whether I'd be able to regain my independence, came and went for the next several days as I struggled to heal, to learn to walk again, and to regain a sense of normalcy.

In hindsight, I think these panicked moments were my ego's way of trying to regain the upper hand. The NDE invited me to live from my heart and soul rather than from my ego. But my ordinary human consciousness felt understandably fearful about the future if it gave up control of my life. After all, one of its self-appointed jobs is safety.

I asked for help through prayer, since that is all I knew at the time. I prayed every day that something would shift. I knew I had to let go of the fear before I could allow the Divine to transform my life, but I had no idea how to do that.

The day before I was discharged from the hospital (day thirteen), I sensed that shift begin. It felt liberating, like a huge weight was lifted off my ego and it could finally rest. I had allowed its fears to overwhelm me, and realized the only way ahead into a positive life was to consciously embrace the gifts and lessons that I had been given during my NDE. I knew I wasn't completely transformed yet, not even close, but I allowed myself to understand that in order to make my life one that would become my version of bliss on Earth, I needed to take responsibility for my choices. That didn't mean I had to do everything alone or all at once, or even perfectly, but it did mean that I had to truly *own* my life, my decisions, and actions from here on out.

Today's Prayer: *Spirit, how can I be more aware and truthful in my life, for myself and those I love?*

One thing I am grateful for this morning:

Optional journaling exercise: Get real with yourself by starting to explore some of your inner truths. Is there a part of your life in which you feel you could take more responsibility? Describe that in your journal, and consider what might be holding you back. Are you afraid? Were you victimized? Are you hobbled by trauma? Do you think you could use some help strengthening this part of your life?

End Your Day

What I am grateful for today:

What didn't go so well today?

What did I learn from that?

Good stuff that happened:

How can I make tomorrow better?

(Day 63) Begin Your Day: _____

"Spirit doesn't want us to put off living special, glorious lives on the promise of a beautiful 'heaven' ahead. Doing that is a waste of all the opportunity that the Creator has given us now on Earth. We are to live our dreams and lives fully, as best as we can, intentionally, with mindfulness, and in glorious homage to love.

"We don't need to wait for heaven to experience love and beauty. We can create our own slice of heaven in our lives right now, and in doing so we can bring a little of it into the lives of others too.

"By choosing to live with love and in beauty, we can bring a little bit of heaven into the lives of those around us. If we choose to live this way, what could happen? Imagine the possibilities.

"Our joy and happiness may infuse others whose lives we touch. We could bring joy into the lives of our families, friends, and even coworkers, besides filling our own lives with joy. We might also inspire others to step out into the unknown and live their lives fully too. We could be the catalyst that a friend needs to leave her abusive husband, to finish a long-ignored university degree, or take that dream trip to Chile. We might inspire others to follow their hearts to bring medical care to a poor village in Africa, or to save a species of hummingbird threatened with extinction. Perhaps our example will inspire a teen who will one day become a Nobel Laureate.

"Who knows where living your life fully will lead you and those you love? You won't know if you don't try." (AFTL, Chapter 16)

Today's Prayer: *How can I help myself live more consciously and fully?*

One thing I am grateful for this morning:

I Intend to make more conscious choices by:

Contemplate this: What would my life look like if I had all of the love, peace, joy, and connection to the Divine that I desire? Then consider what one step can you take toward this life you envision.

End Your Day

What I am grateful for today:

What didn't go so well today?

What did I learn from that?

Good stuff that happened:

How can I make tomorrow better?

Week Nine Review

Use these two pages to summarize your week. What did you experience or learn? Did you have any insights or aha moments? What went well? What would you like more of?

You are the most powerful force for change in your own life.
Only you can decide to move in a new direction.
Only you can make the choice to change your circumstances
And follow the callings of your soul.

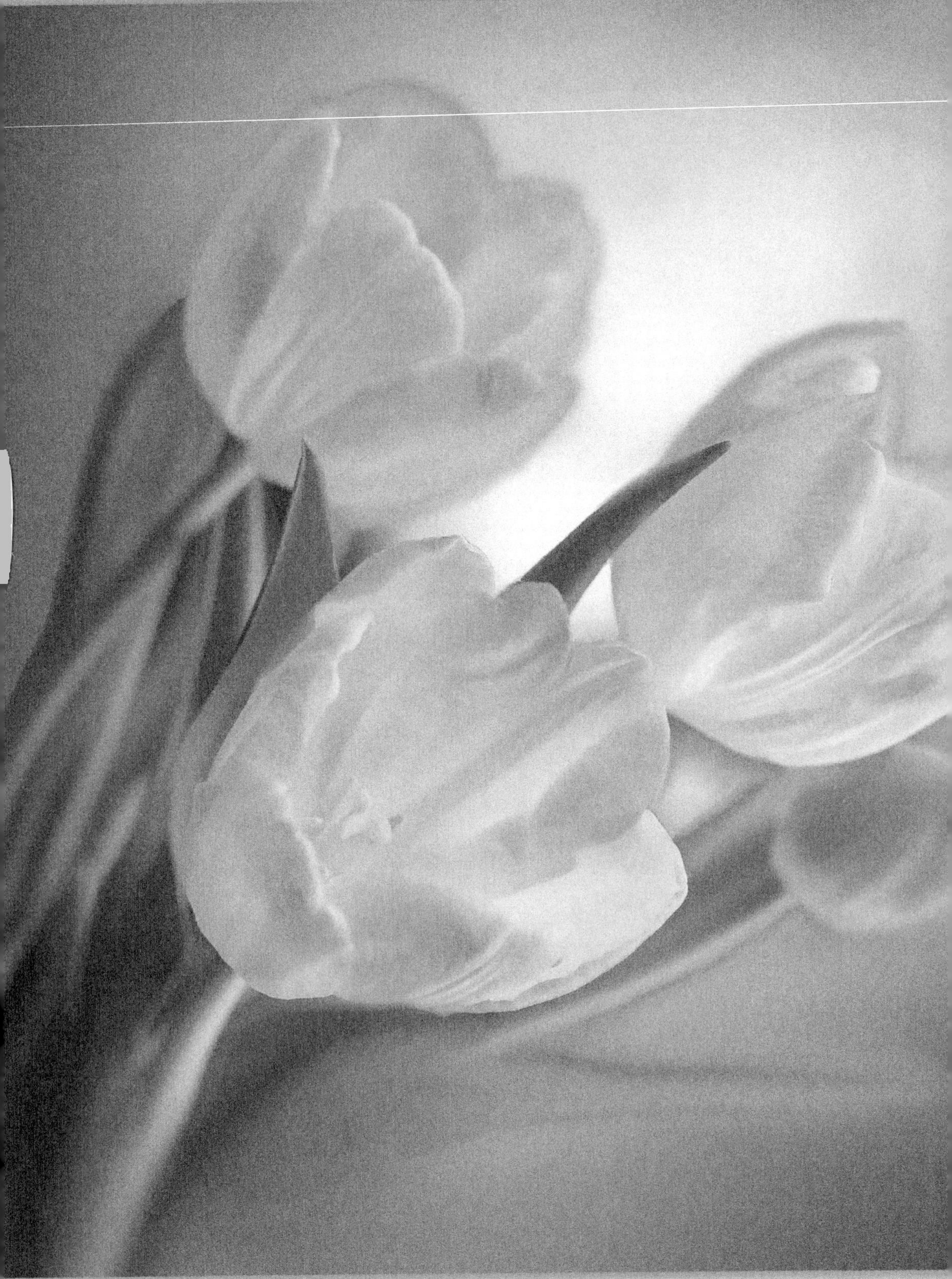

Week Ten: Gratitude

Woohoo! You are now into week ten of this program. Take a moment to think about all of the things you have explored so far: love, compassion, connection, choice, honoring the Earth, loving yourself, and much more. You are doing a great job and I sincerely hope you have enjoyed this journey so far.

This week is all about gratitude, but I am not talking about just saying a simple "thank you" and then going about your day. I treat gratitude as a verb in this program, which means I will ask you to take conscious, positive steps to exercise your gratitude "muscles" this week. My goal is to help you make gratitude a habit.

Why?

Gratitude is really a form of love so actively cultivating it throughout the day will keep you living in those higher state of awareness (i.e., love, compassion, kindness, etc.). Making gratitude a practice will also help you reset your thinking so that you focus on all of the good that you have in your life instead of fixating on a few things that may not be going so well.

Any time you need an attitude reset, and I think we all need one at some point or another, spend a few moments contemplating three things in your life for which you are grateful. These could be as simple as 1) having a warm, safe place to sleep tonight 2) the ability to walk on your own, without assistance and 3) having sight enough to see the sun rise.

You might think these three things are too small to be noteworthy, but let me tell you from personal experience that if you are ever in a situation where you cannot stand on your own, suddenly you will understand how momentous it is to be able to take a step without assistance. Before my accident, I took my own mobility for granted. Not anymore. Just being able to walk without pain every day is a gift for which I am eternally grateful.

This week your challenge is to expand your gratitude practice, make it a regular part of your day, and allow it to bring more love, connection, and positivity into your life. But please do not stop your gratitude practice when this week concludes. I encourage you to allow it to become a part of your life from here, forward, and celebrate the magic it can bring.

(Day 64) Begin Your Day: _____

"Gratitude is one way of demonstrating our love and appreciation back to the Divine for what we have. We might verbally say a prayer of gratitude or "thank you" aloud, but nothing makes a bigger impact spiritually than allowing ourselves to truly feel that gratitude in our hearts.

"To feel love and appreciation is gratitude's purest and deepest form of expression. The power of those feelings emanate from you, much more than words alone. Love transcends all — physical and spiritual.

"We can also choose to live our gratitude daily. Feeling it is wonderful, but transforming that feeling into some positive action is even more powerful. Allowing that gratitude to propel us to do good works in service to others is another tangible expression of love." (AFTL, Chapter 17)

Today's Prayer: *Spirit, thank you for my life and all of the opportunities I am receiving.*

Today I intend to demonstrate my gratitude to others by:

The Gratitude Habit: Think about ways to remind yourself to feel gratitude throughout the day. Remembering in the morning and evening is good, but I also suggest getting into the gratitude habit at other times of the day as well. One easy way is to use meal times as a prompt to consider all of your blessings. Take a few moments before each meal to feel and express your gratitude in that moment.

End Your Day

What I am grateful for today:

What didn't go so well today?

What did I learn from that?

Good stuff that happened:

How can I make tomorrow better?

(Day 65) Begin Your Day: _____

As I write this book in 2021, it has been over seven years since my accident and first NDE. While you might not think that being hit by a truck could lead to anything good, for me it did and I feel grateful for what I learned and how I have evolved as a person.

As one of the chaplains in the hospital observed, it was as if the physical trauma somehow broke open my previously closed-off heart, allowing me to access love and gratitude more deeply than ever before. I had never felt such deep, all-encompassing gratitude before in my life. Prior to my accident, it was more of an intellectual exercise for me. But now I was able to *feel* it deeply, even in my body. That feeling felt like waves of warm, loving, profound love and appreciation.

One memorable time this occurred was during day ten of my hospital stay. A beautiful woman, maybe twenty years my senior, came into my room in order to clean it. We chatted as she cheerfully performed her duties. I noticed that she cleaned with such love and care that it made my heart melt. I felt such deep gratitude for her loving devotion to her work, a job that many people would see as meaningless, that I felt tears sliding down my face.

I thanked her for care in doing her job, but my words could not really express the gratitude I felt that day. I simply had to trust that her heart and soul felt it.

Today's Prayer: *Spirit, thank you for this day, and a new opportunity to live in concert with Divine love.*

Today I am grateful for:

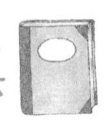

For more super ideas on how to bring gratitude into your life, add **The Gratitude Connection** by Amy Collette to your reading list.

End Your Day

What I am grateful for today:

What didn't go so well today?

What did I learn from that?

Good stuff that happened:

How can I make tomorrow better?

(Day 66) Begin Your Day: _____

For those of us who are not used to truly feeling gratitude in a deep way, doing so might take a little practice. Below is my method. Take some time out of your day and try to locate that feeling of gratitude in your own body with the following contemplation:

Sit alone in a quiet place where you are safe (not operating machinery). Turn off your cell phone and make sure you have no distractions.

Start by trying to feel gratitude for something really big in your life — perhaps for the birth of a child, for the love of a spouse or partner, or for someone saving your life. What comes to mind?

Now close your eyes, and contemplate it.

Think about the enormity of the gift that was given to you. Think about the positive impact it has had, or will have, on your life. Think about all it took for everything to fall into place in order for this event to happen. Allow these thoughts to really hit home. Savor them, and let them reverberate in your heart.

Did anyone make a sacrifice or put something on the line for you when it wasn't required? Why did they do it? Did they have to do it? Or was it simply an act of love and compassion? Think about that, too.

After a few minutes of contemplating the event or the people, do a mental scan of your body. Are you starting to feel something? Are you choked up, with tears in your eyes? Does your heart area feel warm, light, or energized? Are you smiling?

No one is watching, so it's OK to allow any emotions to come out.

If you are feeling some emotion in your body, sit with it for a few minutes and allow the impact of those feelings to wash through you. Revel in that sense of gratitude.

Today's Prayer: *Spirit, I request your assistance and guidance in deeply feeling gratitude for all I have in my life.*

Challenge: Do the above exercise today. Continue it as often as you need to start *feeling* your gratitude in your body.

End Your Day

What I am grateful for today:

Check In: How are you feeling, physically, emotionally, and spiritually?

What didn't go so well today?

What did I learn from that?

Good stuff that happened:

How can I make tomorrow better?

(Day 67) Begin Your Day: _____

"Everything around us has loving energy at its core. And gratitude strengthens love.

"Take a moment to let that sink in; see if you can tease out the connection. Gratitude helps to strengthen the good in the world around us. It's an amplifier to love.

"When we feel grateful, keeping our minds and hearts in that feeling for as long as we can is a form of prayer or meditation. It feels good, and *is* good for us. Gratitude calms our spirits, and can soothe our fears and anxieties. It helps exercise and grow our capacity for love." (AFTL, Chapter 17)

Today's Prayer: *How can I help enhance Divine love and gratitude on this planet?*

One thing I am grateful for this morning:

Today I Intend to demonstrate my gratitude by:

Optional journaling exercise: Brainstorm ways that you can begin to shift towards living more from a place of gratitude, or making gratitude a daily habit. Choose one of these and begin to incorporate it in your life.

Extra Credit: Go back to the "Before You Begin" section on page 12 and review your "Inspires/Energizes Me" list. Choose one topic or activity to incorporate into your week.

End Your Day

What I am grateful for today:

What didn't go so well today?

What did I learn from that?

Good stuff that happened:

How can I make tomorrow better?

(Day 68) Begin Your Day: _____

"During my NDE, my Guide suggested that we try to feel some level of gratitude for what we perceive of as the negatives in our lives, as well as the positives. This can be difficult, especially if the negatives involve the illness or death of someone we love, or some other terrible misfortune. But the negatives can teach us a lot about life, the world, spirituality, and ourselves.

"Try to pull some kernel of learning or gratitude out of each negative event. Are you closer to your father because of his illness? Is your heart more open to love now that you have experienced a loss? Did a terrible accident allow you to reorganize your life in a positive direction? Did you learn a valuable lesson as a result of a negative interaction with a coworker? [*If you are not quite ready to work with this concept right now, go ahead and pass on this reading knowing that you can come back at a later time.*]

"See if you can find something for which you can be grateful in challenging situations. Direct some love toward them if you are able, allowing time for deeper meaning or understanding to come forth. This might be one way to help you uncover any gifts hidden inside those challenges.

"While none of us want to experience difficulties, it's best to avoid hating or fearing them. How we handle the experience, and what we take away from it is often more important than the event itself.

"Send love and appreciation to all of the events in your life, whether easy or difficult. The difficulties allow us an opportunity to grow stronger and deeper in faith, the easy times are gifts to enjoy and savor." (AFTL, Chapter 17)

Today's Prayer: *Spirit, I ask for your guidance in finding any gifts or lessons in this challenging situation:* _____.

One thing I am grateful for this morning:

A challenging event, and what I might learn from it:

Be kind to yourself today. You deserve it! For ideas, check out the "Additional Practices" section near the end of this book (page 247).

End Your Day

What I am grateful for today:

What didn't go so well today?

What did I learn from that?

Good stuff that happened:

How can I make tomorrow better?

Check In: Remember to celebrate your accomplishments and track them in the "Wins" section at the back of the book (page 240).

(Day 69) Begin Your Day: _____

"In *Awakenings from the Light*, I wrote about how the energy we project outward, we eventually get back in some way. This works for the love that is gratitude too.

"While we might actually *get* more coming back into our own lives when we truly *feel* that love and appreciation of gratitude, we're asked not to allow the pursuit of material goods to be the sole reason we allow ourselves to feel grateful. Material goods are fleeting at best. Our garbage dumps are filled with all of the things we simply had to have just a few years ago.

"But spiritual love outlasts material goods. A strong, loving relationship on Earth can last a human lifetime and weather countless storms. Allowing ourselves to feel and express love and appreciation to others can enhance these relationships and thus bring us more of what many of us truly desire — deep connectedness and closeness to others." (AFTL, Chapter 17)

Today's Prayer: *Thank you for allowing me the perfect opportunity for the learning and growth I most need right now.*

One thing I am grateful for this morning:

Today I Intend to give back to others by:

Contemplate this: Focus on the "now moment" in your life. Be truly grateful for what you have, even as you work toward a brighter future.

Extra Credit: Go back to the "Before You Begin" section (page 13) and reach out and connect with someone on your "People I love" list.

End Your Day

What I am grateful for today:

What didn't go so well today?

What did I learn from that?

Good stuff that happened:

How can I make tomorrow better?

(Day 70) Begin Your Day: _____

"Channel some of your gratitude back to yourself, too. After all, you deserve love just as much as anyone else! Be grateful to yourself for working on achieving or maintaining a healthy body, mind, and spirit. Be grateful to yourself for having the persistence to achieve a goal or to emotionally support a friend in need. Find ways every day to feel gratitude towards *you*.

"Why?

"This kind of self-appreciation shows Spirit that you love this amazing creation that is *you*. It also sends some of that positive energy back in to your own life. Appreciate the health that you do have, even if you could feel a little better. Appreciate the strength that you have, your wit, your sense of humor, whatever uniqueness that is yours. All of it. Remember that your gratitude and appreciation will strengthen anything you direct it towards, including your own abilities and talents.

"Love and appreciate your body, every glorious inch of it. Be grateful for the marvel that it is: how thousands, millions, or billions of components work together seamlessly to make up you.

"Appreciate your mind and emotions — both their whole and "broken" parts.

"Appreciate your spiritual center — for it is the place where you most strongly feel the connection to Spirit." (AFTL, Chapter 17)

Today's Prayer: *Spirit, thank you for the gifts of my body, mind, and soul so that I can fully experience and appreciate this Divine universe!*

One thing I am grateful for this morning:

Things I am grateful for in myself:

Contemplate a difficult relationship in your life. Find something for which you can be grateful as a result of this relationship or its challenges. Spend some time thinking about the other person. Is there anything you have learned, or can learn, from interacting with him or her? Can you find something positive to take away from this difficult relationship? Do you have something in common, or perhaps there is one thing you admire in him or her. If so, spend a few moments feeling grateful for what you've learned.

End Your Day

What I am grateful for today:

What didn't go so well today?

What did I learn from that?

Good stuff that happened:

How can I make tomorrow better?

Week Ten Review

Use these two pages to summarize your week. What did you experience or learn? Did you have any insights or aha moments? What went well? What would you like more of?

Allow yourself to inspire
others by being of service.
Helping others is a beautifully simple way to
spread Divine love.

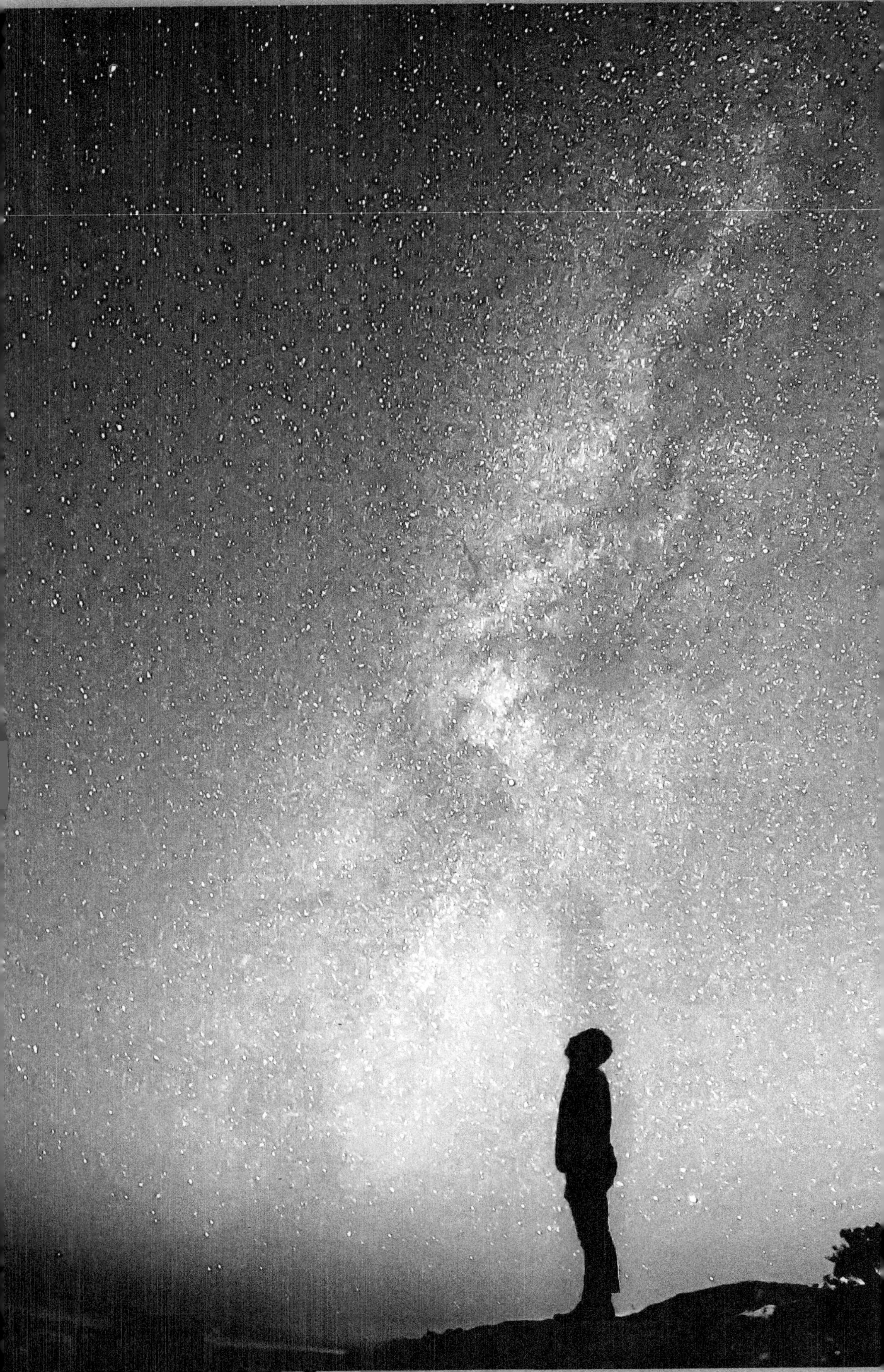

Week Eleven: Expanding Your Perspective

How would you react if I told you that what you *think you know* about this physical world may be wrong? What if I told you that "physical reality" is not really physical at all, and that our scientists still do not understand over 95% of the universe? And what would you say if I told you that some very savvy people, scientists and spiritually minded people alike, are convinced that what we perceive of as "real" is simply an illusion, or perhaps even some bizarre simulation?

Do you think I might be a tad crazy?

Perhaps I am, but if so I am in some terrific company!

This week I will begin to challenge you to expand your thinking in a variety of areas, encourage you to consider pushing past the boundaries of your comfort zones, and question what you think you know about yourself and the universe. I have enjoyed putting this week's readings together and I sincerely hope you have fun exploring with me.

The world you live in is full of wonder, possibility, beauty, love, and just plain weird things that should not happen in a purely material, mechanistic, or clockwork universe. But we now know that our universe is anything but mechanistic. Instead, at its heart it is a quantum universe of energy, probability, and possibility. And in my view, this quantum universe of energy is built of a construct of Divine love and intention.

Nothing over the next seven days is intended to negate any spiritual beliefs you may have, nor is it a deep-dive into scientific ideas. Some of the readings and practices might challenge you, though, or even enhance or expand your spiritual beliefs. Ultimately I would love for you to come away from this next week with the willingness to be curious, to question your thoughts and beliefs, to gently question others' ideas in a healthy way, and to be open to wonder. I hope I can help you expand the boundaries of your thinking a little too, not just from a scientific perspective, but from a spiritual one as well. I give you permission to daydream again like you may have done when you were a child, to play with seemingly weird ideas (including quantum physics), and to be open to expanding your awareness and consciousness.

(Day 71) Begin Your Day: _____

One of the most amazing gifts from having an NDE, or any other spiritually transformative experience, is coming away with the realization that we are more than just this one little person living a relatively humble life right here and now. We are much more than our fears and insecurities, our struggles, our successes, our anxieties, and our losses. We are more than someone's parent, child, friend, or employee. And we are much more than just our human selves.

We learn that our true selves are essentially infinite consciousness and energy; that we are expansive, powerful, creative, and connected to everyone and everything. We learn that we are more than this life we are living, and that our capacity to love, and be loved, is beyond our ability to comprehend it with the human mind.

We also come to understand that we can bring at least some of this spiritual love into our lives here on Earth. We come away with the understanding that we are intimately connected with the Divine in each and every moment, and that the universe of which we are a part is, quite simply, extraordinary. It is more extraordinary and diverse than even our most brilliant scientists can dream. More importantly, we come away from a spiritual experience with the knowledge that we too are extraordinary. We don't have to live crippled by lack, limitation, and fear, not with these marvelous and expansive souls at our cores, and not when we are supported in every moment by Divine love and presence.

Today's Prayer: *Spirit, help me see and live from my truest, most expansive eternal self.*

One thing I am grateful for this morning:

Today I Intend to:

Practice for the week: Be a Pollyanna. Expect to see the good in the world around you. Search out good news on the internet and share it with others. When you see a kind act, feel gratitude for seeing it. When you see evidence of love, smile and say a silent thanks. When you bring your awareness to the good around you, you retrain your brain so that seeing and celebrating the good in life becomes your new normal over time.

End Your Day

What I am grateful for today:

What didn't go so well today?

What did I learn from that?

Good stuff that happened:

How can I make tomorrow better?

(Day 72a) Begin Your Day: _____

The non-science option (turn the page to see a science option for today):

Relax into quiet moments and allow Divine love to work its magic on your heart and mind. Let go of any need you might have for drama or anxiety.

Breathe in Divine love. Breathe out quiet and calmness. Know that you are a very real part of this Divine, love-filled universe.

Avoid concerning yourself so much with what other people are doing or thinking. Instead, pay attention in the present moment to strengthening love and peace in your own life. You must make an effort to nurture love and peace so they can grow and blossom for yourself and those close to you. Trust me when I say that you *can* cultivate more of both *because they are already a part of you* and your connection to the Divine.

Above all, always remember that you are a precious, beloved, and integral part of this limitless, Divine, and conscious universe.

Today's Prayer: *Spirit, help me more clearly hear and understand Your wisdom and the wisdom of my own soul.*

One thing I am grateful for this morning:

Today I Intend to:

Love is your link to the true Divine, or what I call the field of Divine love. Choosing to manifest love in your life as much as you can strengthens the field of love around you, and thus your connection to the spiritual realm. When you choose to cultivate love in your life, in all its forms, you are learning to walk the path peace, joy, and connection.

End Your Day

What I am grateful for today:

What didn't go so well today?

What did I learn from that?

Good stuff that happened:

How can I make tomorrow better?

(Day 72b) Begin Your Day: _____

The science option (see the prior page for the non-science option):

Let me share a mind-bending thought to start your day: the concept of *time* as an immutable arrow moving from the past to the future probably does not actually exist the way we like to believe. In fact, modern science tells us that there may be no arrow of time at all.

Allow me bend your mind a little more: there is no such thing as the "smallest particle" of physical matter. At the smallest scale, physical matter is not actually made of bits of even smaller pieces of matter. When we dive down and look at *stuff* at the smallest scale, what we really observe could be termed *energy*, and even more bizarre, *probabilities* and *possibilities*. Even deeper into the bizarre, scientists have demonstrated that at the smallest scales, these little bits of energy and probability can be influenced by an observer. The observer of an experiment that investigates this smallest aspect of reality absolutely changes what the experiment shows her, just by her expectation or intent. In other words, *the observer of one of these experiments sees what they expect to see.*

Chew on that for a moment.

The last 120 or more years of scientific investigation continue to show us just how weird and wonder-filled this universe is. At times, our physical reality seems more akin to the *holodeck* from *Star Trek* (a holographic simulation of reality), than a purely physical universe.

The reality in which we live is *anything but* physical matter, and to me that is exactly what makes it so interesting.

Today's Prayer: *Spirit, help me more clearly hear and understand Your wisdom and the wisdom inherent in this universe.*

One thing I am grateful for this morning:

Today I Intend to:

Would you like to learn more cutting-edge ideas about reality? Read books (or watch videos) by Dr. Brian Greene, but especially *The Elegant Universe* and *The Fabric of the Cosmos*.

End Your Day

What I am grateful for today:

What didn't go so well today?

What did I learn from that?

Good stuff that happened:

How can I make tomorrow better?

(Day 73) Begin Your Day: _____

Let's dive in to the subject of time a little deeper today.

One of the strangest things that I was taught during my NDE was that the passage of time as we view it here in our physical reality is an illusion. It does not actually exist at the spiritual level the way it does here. In fact, both time and space were meaningless concepts to the beings of light with whom I interacted. I am not the only experiencer to come back with this understanding, though. In fact, it is a common thread that runs through accounts of NDEs, out-of-body experiences, and similar spiritual encounters.

My spiritual guides were adamant that the passage of time that we sense here is merely a *construct* of our physical reality, and my stay in the afterlife demonstrated that to me. During what amounted to perhaps the equivalent of two to three months I spent in there in the afterlife, I saw no cues as to time passing. No sunrises or sunsets. No feelings of the need to eat or sleep. Everything was *now*, never changing, and perhaps even eternal.

Let us consider the scientific viewpoint for a moment. Modern physics also tells us that what we experience as the arrow of time may simply be an illusion, and time itself is not absolute (the same for everyone in the universe) but instead seems to be different depending on your circumstances. So science and spirituality are not that far apart after all, at least when it comes to the passage of time.

But who cares? Does this do you any good in your life right now?

What if the passage of time were merely an illusion? *What if* you could somehow contact a past version of yourself and give him or her a message? Would you do it? What would you say? And how might it change your life?

Today's Prayer: *Spirit, I ask for your help in aligning myself to your love and light, so that I can be an example of peace and connection for others.*

One thing I am grateful for this morning:

Challenge: Create a little good for a past version of yourself. Pick a time in your life when you could have used some love or encouragement. Then get your mind as quiet as possible with your favorite form of meditation, prayer, or quiet mind activity. Next, in your inner eye form a picture of your younger self. Be as detailed as you can. When you have the image in your mind, give that prior version of you the messages of love and encouragement you so desperately needed at that time. When you feel you have communicated as much as possible, simply open your eyes and come back to the present moment.

End Your Day

What I am grateful for today:

What didn't go so well today?

What did I learn from that?

Good stuff that happened:

How can I make tomorrow better?

Extra Credit: Go back to the "Before You Begin" section on page 12 and review your "Inspires/Energizes Me" list. Choose one topic or activity to incorporate into your week.

(Day 74) Begin Your Day: _____

I have a friend, Megan, whose husband, David, is a pretty cool guy. He's an engineer who doesn't spend much time contemplating all of this "woo-woo" stuff in which his wife and I are interested. It's not that he discounts it, but it is not the focus of his life. David is a bit of a man's man: athletic, outdoorsy, and is not into fashion or cosmetics.

Even with our slightly different approaches to life, David and I are cordial to each other when I travel to Colorado to visit his wife. And while I like and respect David, we do not have a deep friendship or recurring communication on our own.

One January morning several months after I last visited the couple, I was preparing to record a video interview that would air in a few months' time. I applied my normal makeup routine of mineral foundation, powder, and blush. Then I took out some lipstick I had purchased at the drugstore a few days prior. Up until that time I did not often use lipstick, disliking the way it felt on my skin. So of course I did not keep any on hand.

I had not given the lipstick much thought when I purchased it but now as I was about to apply it I silently asked myself, "I wonder if this stuff is toxic?" No one else was in the room with me to ask and since I didn't have any time to research lipstick on my own before the interview, my question remained unanswered. With the interview just a few minutes away, I turned the tube over in my hand, looked at it for a moment, then decided to go ahead and use it since I did not have another option. The interview went well and by the end of it I had completely forgotten about my lipstick question.

The next morning I checked my email and noticed a message from David. To put this into perspective, David had only emailed me once before, a few years prior, with some information about a medical condition we once discussed. He had not emailed me since that time so to receive any communication from him was unexpected to say the least. Additionally, neither he nor Megan knew about the interview I had recorded the day before.

In his email, David had written a few short lines suggesting that I check out recent health research on makeup in general, and lipstick in particular. I was stunned. What in the world was going on? First of all, David was not at all into women's fashion and cosmetics, so to have him sending me random articles on makeup shocked me. Second, how in the world could he possibly have known that I was just thinking about this very same topic less than 12 hours before he sent his email?

The first article he included was titled something like, "Which Lipsticks are Toxic, and Why?" One of those crawling little sensations ran up my spine. I bet you know that sensation — you get it when you receive confirmation, once again, that reality isn't exactly what you think it is. How in the world had David, who was living 1500 miles away and with whom I had no contact for months, suddenly decided that I needed to see this report on lipstick toxicity just a few hours after I had asked myself that seemingly innocent question?

Mere chance? Probably not, especially since this kind of thing happens to me several times a month. What do you think? Your exercise for today is to think about what happened to me, and then write down any similar experiences you have had.

Today's Prayer: *Spirit, how can I better tune in to my friends and family?*

End Your Day

What I am grateful for today:

What didn't go so well today?

What did I learn from that?

Good stuff that happened:

How can I make tomorrow better?

(Day 75) Begin Your Day: _____

What is the nature of what we consider "physical reality?" Sometimes it seems we have as many answers to this question as there are people on the planet. But among those like me who have died and then been brought back to life, there is a common theme in our experiences: what we call physical reality is, in part, a constructed "classroom" for our soul-essences to learn and grow. It is a state of existence that is an illusion, at least from the perspective of our spiritual selves.

Cutting-edge scientists are also increasingly vocal about the idea that what we perceive of as a physical universe is, in fact, an incredibly sophisticated hologram or illusion. Dr. Niels Bohr, one of the leading scientists of the last century, was adamant that matter (i.e., physical "stuff") as we know it, does not really exist. Dr. Albert Einstein said essentially the same thing over a half century ago. As time passes, more and more of our greatest scientific and spiritual thinkers alike are converging on the idea that the world around us is not really made of physical stuff at all, especially when we look at the smallest levels of our physical existence.

But let's get practical for a moment. No matter what physical reality ultimately turns out to be, the fact is that we are here, now. We have lives to live, perhaps things to learn or accomplish, and families to raise. How can we go forward in a universe in which reality is not quite as straightforward as it appears at first glance?

Take that knowledge and carry it with you as a source of strength, fearlessness, awareness, and presence as you live your life. But continue live your life. Enjoy your time here. Learn what you can. Do good things. Remain curious and ask questions, especially of yourself. And above all, pay attention to the reality that you create for yourself every day through your thoughts, beliefs, words, and intent.

Today's Prayer: *I ask for Divine guidance in making my time in the physical realm one of beauty, peace, love, and fun.*

One thing I am grateful for this morning:

Today I Intend to:

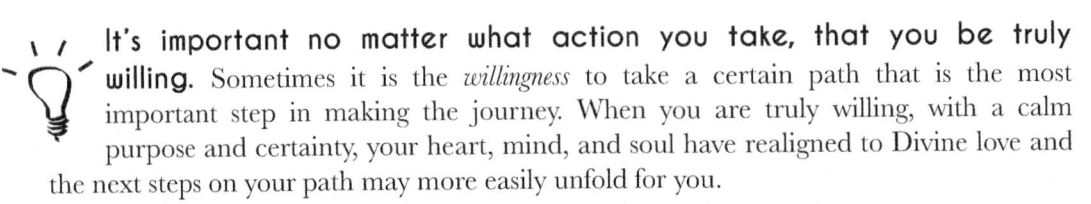

It's important no matter what action you take, that you be truly willing. Sometimes it is the *willingness* to take a certain path that is the most important step in making the journey. When you are truly willing, with a calm purpose and certainty, your heart, mind, and soul have realigned to Divine love and the next steps on your path may more easily unfold for you.

End Your Day

What I am grateful for today:

What didn't go so well today?

What did I learn from that?

Good stuff that happened:

How can I make tomorrow better?

(Day 76) Begin Your Day: _____

It's easy for us to overlook the beauty and divinity of Earth, especially if we are longing for the opportunity to return to our spiritual home. While the spiritual realm is an incredible state of love and connection, the reason that I create the paintings that I do is that this physical life, here and now, is a blessed, wonder-filled realm of love, beauty, and opportunity too. I want to show this love and beauty to everyone through my art.

I know that one of the reasons that I am here is to be a voice on canvas for the beauty all around us, right here and now. I want to show you how amazing and beautiful *you all are*, and how beautiful and full of promise this world is. Through *all* of my work, I hope I can help you appreciate the great gifts you have, and bring some light to your life.

Take a moment to look out a window. Find a tree, clouds, a bird, a dog or cat, or whatever is available. I don't care if the scene is "pretty" or "ugly" since those are simply human judgements anyway. Take a look at the world beyond your immediate surroundings for a moment. Deeply observe without judgment. You are seeing the Divine take form, right in front of you.

Sit with that for a moment.

Right here, right now, this is heaven.

If you look around and don't like what you see, remember that you have the power to work toward making things better. Or you can decide to shift your attitude about it. The choice, as always, is yours.

Today's Prayer: *Spirit, I ask for your guidance to see the true beauty of this planet, and in my life.*

One thing I am grateful for this morning:

Today I Intend to:

Do you see the beauty and love that is here around you, or is your mind focused instead on all that is wrong? Take one step toward seeing the beauty around you today: go for a walk in nature and appreciate its sights and sounds; look at pictures of beautiful landscapes on the internet or in a book; go into your garden and feel grateful for the abundance of life you find; buy some cut flowers for your home. Take one small step today to appreciate the beauty that is right outside your door.

End Your Day

What I am grateful for today:

What didn't go so well today?

What did I learn from that?

Good stuff that happened:

How can I make tomorrow better?

Extra Credit: Go back to the "Before You Begin" section (page 13) and reach out and connect with someone on your "People I love" list.

(Day 77) Begin Your Day: _____

Consider this: the only things you can actually control are your own thoughts, beliefs, reactions, actions, and words. How does that feel to you? Do you believe that? Why or why not?

Think about it a different way — you often cannot control an outside event, like a hot water heater suddenly breaking, but you *can* control how you think about it, react to it, act afterwards, and the words you speak about it. If you allow your mind to continuously loop through how unfair it is that your hot water heater broke and that the universe is out to get you, you will waste precious time and energy *angsting* about it rather than taking the needed steps just to fix it.

Fretting over the event itself, especially one that you could not control or is done and cannot be changed, does not solve anything. In fact, it creates more stress for you.

You absolutely *can* choose a different approach, one that will create a more positive future state. You can choose to think and act differently, which itself just might bring your solution into focus.

Today's Prayer: *Spirit, today I am open to understanding the true message in challenging events and situations.*

One thing I am grateful for this morning:

Today I Intend to:

Contemplate a challenging event. Did you have any control over it happening? Is there something positive you can take from the situation? Can you learn something as a result of what happened? If you need to make a course correction, maybe your new path will be better than the one you originally laid out for yourself. Think about ways you can go forward in a more positive direction.

End Your Day

What I am grateful for today:

What didn't go so well today?

What did I learn from that?

Good stuff that happened:

How can I make tomorrow better?

Divine love is a blessing, the core energy that ties us all together. It spans all of time and space.

Week Eleven Review

Use these two pages to summarize your week. What did you experience or learn? Did you have any insights or aha moments? What went well? What would you like more of?

> The ultimate prayer is simply love.

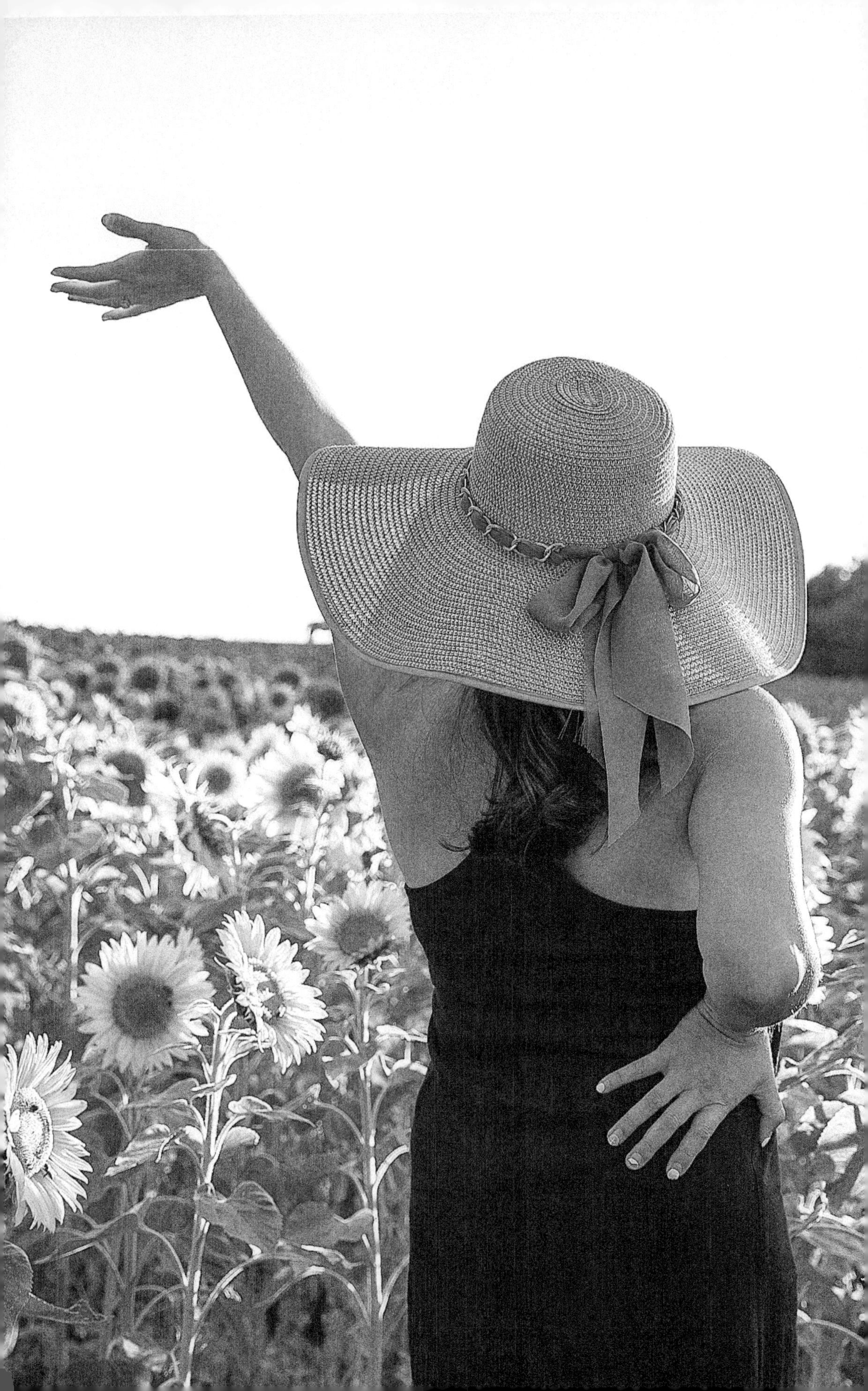

Week Twelve: Uniquely YOU!

Congratulations on making it to the last week of this three month program. By now, you have delved into a variety of topics from Divine love to the nature of reality. I hope your comfort zones have been expanded and you have a new awareness of how small, daily practices can positively impact your life.

This week is all about you: your gifts, talents, and unique soul-essence. I will ask you to envision your ideal life, at the same time giving you permission to have fun, explore your talents, and share your uniqueness with the world.

The world desperately needs you to fully embrace and live your glorious life as a unique creation; to show up every day, owning who you really are and sharing that with everyone around you[7]. The world does not need more reality television and social media clones; we need your talents, your unique views of the world, your crazy-brilliant ideas, and every bit of hope and vision you can muster. We need you to be curious, ask questions, and fearlessly investigate and share new ideas. But the most important thing that the world needs is for you to *own* your powerful, love-filled, spiritual essence, while at the same time being an advocate for others to do the same.

Your time to shine is now.

Let's all shine together so that we can bring more light to this world.

Once again I invite you to draw, paint, sculpt, knit, sew, dance, or create music that reflects what you feel or comes to you as insights or inspiration this week. Give free reign to your creativity and unique soul this week.

---

[7] As long as you do no harm to yourself or others.

(Day 78) Begin Your Day: _____

You have a unique suite of gifts that makes you special, and in turn makes your life unique. Using these gifts to the best of your abilities is an expression of gratitude and love back to Spirit and the universe. Step out of your comfort zones and take a chance on yourself in order to make your life full, complete, and wonderfully extraordinary.

When you do that, when you live fully and share your gifts, your soul rejoices. So too does Spirit. It is as if you are sending a huge thank you out to the universe. With your life you are saying: I love what I have and I am using my gifts to their fullest, in love, in joy, and in beauty. Thank you!

Set free your thinking and begin to release any limiting beliefs you may have about yourself. See what kinds of visions you can generate for your own life.

Follow your heart and see where it leads. It may just bring you to wondrous things!

Today's Prayer: *Spirit, thank you for helping me see the special nature of my own unique gifts.*

One thing I am grateful for this morning:

Today I Intend to:

Practice for the week: Your Miraculous Life and World. Refer to this exercise in the "Additional Practices" section near the end of the book (page 251), and devote regular time to it this week.

End Your Day

What I am grateful for today:

What didn't go so well today?

What did I learn from that?

Good stuff that happened:

How can I make tomorrow better?

(Day 79) Begin Your Day: _____

In order to create your most authentic life, I encourage you to be open to releasing any attachments you may have to living according to society's ideal. Spirit doesn't expect you to be anyone other than your true self. Learn, yes. Adapt, yes. Grow, yes. But until you finally leave this planet, you are here as an imperfect human with a sometimes-challenging life. You will mess up, yes, but you will also succeed and achieve. And you will have fun, love as best you can, learn, grow, create, explore, inspire, and then move on to your next adventure.

But it's too easy to get caught up in the desire to to live someone else's idea of a good life. We often want to be adored, esteemed, respected, followed, loved, cared for, successful, wealthy, or beautiful. But in striving for these things, we wear ourselves out trying to be what we think other people want us to be.

But that's not what Spirit wants for us, and ultimately, that is not what our souls crave.

We were born here as unique individuals for a reason: to experience the joys and struggles of uniqueness. To learn how to be our truest, deepest selves. To create a unique life that is meaningful for us. To love each other. To learn. To experience. To grow. And to love who we are as we were made. In channeling our own uniqueness we pay homage to the One who created it.

We're not meant to be perfect. We are meant to be us.

You are not meant to be perfect. You are meant to be *you*.

Today's Prayer: *Thank you for making me unique and allowing me to know and live my truth.*

One thing I am grateful for this morning:

Today I Intend to:

The gifts you have are yours to share, and in developing and living those gifts, you forward Divine love and wisdom on this planet. Think about your unique gifts, talents, interests, and passions. What are they? Jot them down in a notebook or computer file if you haven't already. Re-read your list and figure out ways you can dedicate more time or energy to developing one or two that call out to you.

End Your Day

What I am grateful for today:

Check In: How are you feeling, physically, emotionally, and spiritually?

What didn't go so well today?

What did I learn from that?

Good stuff that happened:

How can I make tomorrow better?

Extra Credit: Go back to the "Before You Begin" section (page 13) and review your "I Want to Learn" list. Choose one of them and take a step toward learning it. Locate a book, website, or class that will get you started.

(Day 80) Begin Your Day: _____

This life is the only opportunity you have to live fully as the person you are now.
    This is it.
    What are you waiting for?

When we're young children, we tend to live life simply *as we are*. We usually live from an intuitive or heart-centered space, just being our genuine, authentic selves. But as we grow, oftentimes our parents, circumstances, and society begin to influence us away from our innate inner truths. In his book *The Four Agreements*, don Miguel Ruiz calls this process "domestication." Not knowing any better, we allow other people to influence the image we have of who we are and what we want for our lives.

    Some of us who are very strong, or strongly in tune with our inner truths, resist this process and have an easier time living life on our own terms. Many people aren't strong enough to resist, though, and go through years of living falsely before realizing they have gotten off track. Sadly, some people never understand, and remain unhappy inside but never know why.

    It's OK to notice the expectations others may have of you, but the key is to avoid allowing them to overwhelm your own, most authentic self.

Today's Prayer: *Spirit, my path to a full and meaningful life starts now. I take responsibility for creating the life of my dreams!*

One thing I am grateful for this morning:

Today I Intend to:

Challenge: Avoid all recreational screen time, media, and social media today (except anything strictly related to your work or business). Instead, take time for you and/or your family: read a book that interests you, talk to a friend, journal about your life, go for a walk, devote time to one of your talents or interests, or perhaps watch the sun set.

End Your Day

What I am grateful for today:

What didn't go so well today?

What did I learn from that?

Good stuff that happened:

How can I make tomorrow better?

(Day 81) Begin Your Day: _____

When you give voice to the truly creative, unique person that you are, your soul sings a song of joy and gratitude back to the Divine. Loving and appreciating yourself and living the truth of who you are as a light-filled spiritual being, might just be the best form of gratitude you can give to Spirit in any given moment.

In being yourself, in accepting your limits while loving to the best of your abilities, you are a perfect expression of the Divine spark that rests inside of you.

You don't need to channel a star being from the tenth dimension to live a fulfilled life here on Earth. Spend more time channeling your own creative self. You have a gateway to peace and happiness inside of you. It is the beauty, wisdom, and connection to your Higher Power and your own creative, loving, and magnificent soul.

Today's Prayer: *I desire Divine help in uncovering my unique gifts and talents that will allow me to bring my own deep creativity to this world.*

One thing I am grateful for this morning:

Today I Intend to:

don Miguel Ruiz's's *The Four Agreements,* is a simple yet powerful book for helping you enhance and deepen your spiritual awareness and sense of inner peace.

End Your Day

What I am grateful for today:

What didn't go so well today?

What did I learn from that?

Good stuff that happened:

How can I make tomorrow better?

(Day 82) Begin Your Day: _____

At your core, you are a spiritual being of love and light. When you believe this in your heart and start to live as if it were true, you align yourself more strongly with the Divine universe. Allow any obstacles you have to this love to simply fall away. Your sense of peace and love will grow as a result.

We are all equal children of the Divine. When you remember that, or when you make a conscious choice to believe it, then you will begin to know Divine grace in your life.

Living in peace and love on Earth is a practice, something you can choose to cultivate every day. It doesn't matter if you believe that you failed today, tomorrow is another opportunity to choose to align with love. In truth, you cannot really fail as long as you learn, grow, and commit to doing your best.

The light and love of the Divine is always there for you to call on, for it is a part of you. Ask and it truly is given, but be open and grateful for what is given. Spirit may gift you not with what you desire, but with what you truly *need* in order to continue on with the next part of your life.

Today's Prayer: *I ask for Spirit's blessing and guidance to see the light and love in everyone around me.*

One thing I am grateful for this morning:

Today I Intend to:

Contemplate: How can I be an angel for someone else today? How can I be an angel for myself?

Extra Credit: Go back to the "Before You Begin" section (page 13) and reach out and connect with someone on your "People I love" list.

End Your Day

What I am grateful for today:

What didn't go so well today?

What did I learn from that?

Good stuff that happened:

How can I make tomorrow better?

(Day 83) Begin Your Day: _____

Message from Nancy's spiritual guides:

You are the most powerful force for change in your own life. Only you can take the wheel and move your course into another direction. Ultimately, only you can change your circumstances and in so doing, affect the circumstances of others too. Only you.

But you have within you all you need to make it happen.

You are the bright star in your own little universe. You are the one shining the light into your world. The Divine is there in your heart, yes, but you are the way through which Divine work is done in your world.

You.

Each *you* is important for together, you span the globe.

You *can* be a force for change. Believe it. And be open to believing in your own power to change your life for the better.

Today's Prayer: *Spirit, today I surround myself in your field of Divine love. I ask your help in making the changes that will bring me to living my best and highest good.*

One thing I am grateful for this morning:

Today I Intend to:

Remember that a spiritual journey takes as long as it takes. Time is a human constraint, not a spiritual one, so relax and allow your journey to unfold in its own unique way without stress and expectation of any particular outcome or timeframe.

End Your Day

What I am grateful for today:

What didn't go so well today?

What did I learn from that?

Good stuff that happened:

How can I make tomorrow better?

(Day 84) Begin Your Day: _____

"Life shouldn't be all seriousness, struggle, and self-improvement. One of the things I took away from my near-death experience is to enjoy my days on Earth as much as I can. I hope you do, too.

"Do what you love to the best of your abilities. This is one of the ingredients for an inspired life.

"Listen to the callings of your heart, for in it is the key to happiness and fulfillment. It's one of God's way of speaking directly to you.

"Know that there is more than just this life, that Spirit is there for you any time, and your life on Earth is precious and wonderful.

"Laugh. Dance. Ski. Swim. Watch the sun set. Dip your toes in the ocean. Play with your kids. Enjoy your pets. Gaze in awe at mountains. Fall in love. Help a friend. Open your heart and sing your gratitude to Spirit for this glorious life you've been given." (AFTL, Chapters 22 and 23)

Today's Prayer: *Thank you for helping me find fun, joy, and laughter in my life today.*

One thing I am grateful for this morning:

Today I Intend to:

> **Jot down some of the things that bring joy, laughter, or fun into your life.** Next, commit to taking a little bit of time each day for at least one of them.

End Your Day

What I am grateful for today:

What didn't go so well today?

What did I learn from that?

Good stuff that happened:

How can I make tomorrow better?

This is it. This is your life. What are you waiting for?

Week Twelve Review

Use these two pages to summarize your week. What did you experience or learn? Did you have any insights or aha moments? What went well? What would you like more of?

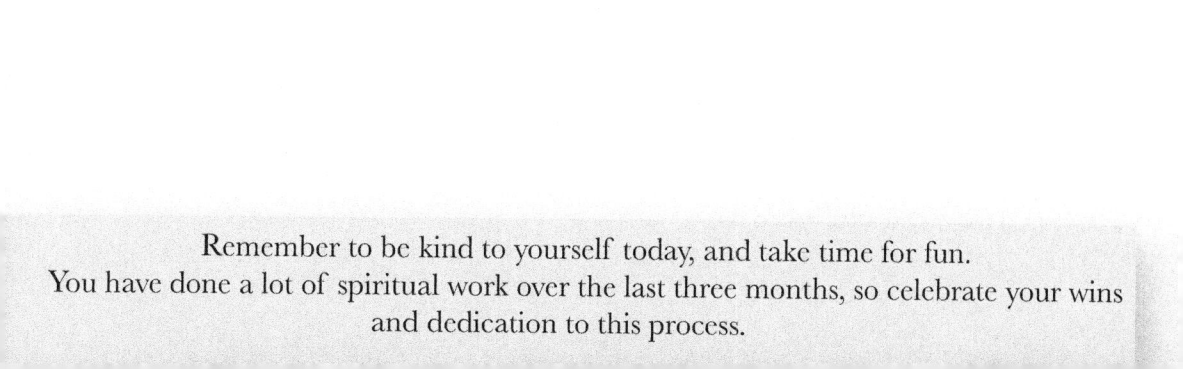

Remember to be kind to yourself today, and take time for fun.
You have done a lot of spiritual work over the last three months, so celebrate your wins
and dedication to this process.

Three Month Review

"I still remember every detail of the crash, being in the hospital, and the recovery process. Friends have said they thought remembering everything would be too traumatic. They contend that they would want to have amnesia if it happened to them. While I didn't have a choice in whether I remembered or not, I now see those memories as a blessing.

"Why?

"They allowed me a first glimpse into the nature of my existence on Earth, of the reality of my spirituality, and that I have nothing to fear in dying.

"More important than the memories of the accident are the ones from the Guide I met, and the information she passed on to me. I remember the love, the beauty, peace, harmony, and the loving Presence that suffused everything there. I carry it with me still. It might get a little lost in the humanness of daily life, but it's there when I consciously choose to call on it.

"That little bit of heaven is as real to me as sitting here at this computer, typing. Actually, it's more real.

"That place, state of reality, or whatever you choose to call it, is our true home. It is where our souls ultimately belong. There, we are loved beyond all reasoning. We are connected to each other in ways we can't conceive of here on Earth. Spirit's love suffuses us in ways that would cripple our human brains to try to understand.

"Whether you choose to believe in heaven or not, spiritual love is there for you all of the time. If what I experienced was nothing more than encountering the depths and truths of my own humanity, the knowledge and insights I gained are worth the pain I endured. But in my own internal wisdom, and from the experiences of others like me, I believe and trust that my experience was somehow more than that. I did come face-to-face with my inner truths, but I think I touched on something more profound and mysterious.

"Do I know *for sure* what comes after this life?

"No. But I had a pretty good glimpse.

"As a scientist, I can only say that I experienced something profound and mysterious that has changed my life forever. While I have a hint of what's to come, and got a glimmer of something profoundly spiritual, I can't explain it in scientific terms. It's simply profoundly mysterious and awe-inspiring, and I'm OK leaving it at that." (AFTL, Chapter 20)

What I learned and how I changed over the last three months:

Celebrate your wins. *If you haven't done so yet, go through this book and copy all of your "wins" to the celebration pages starting on page 240, or to a separate journal you dedicate to your wins. Having all of your successes listed in one place makes it easier to review them in the future when you need an emotional boost.*

Three Month Progress Check

Did I create more of what I wanted over the last three months?

What I accomplished:

How am I feeling overall right now? (Life, family, work, etc.)

Did I spend time doing what inspires or energizes me?

Did I spend more time with people I love?

Did I spend more time doing things I enjoy?

What I learned over the last three months:

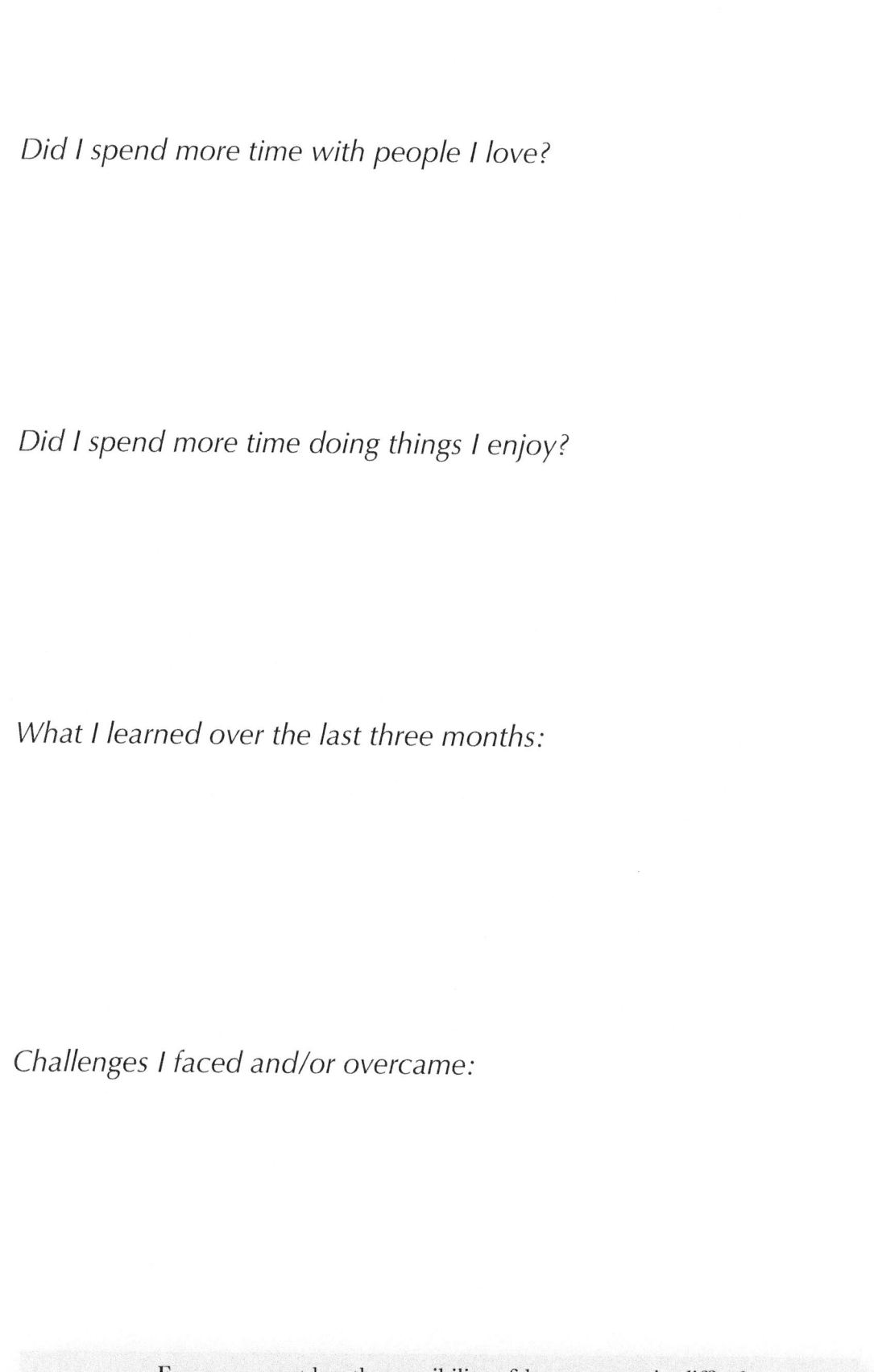

Challenges I faced and/or overcame:

Every moment has the possibility of beauty, even in difficulty.
Every moment is an opportunity to learn, to grow, to love, or to take an action
that advances you toward your ideals, dreams, and goals.

2 Next Steps on Your Journey

Thank you so much for taking the time and energy to spend your days with me over the past several weeks. I hope this journey has opened you up to ideas, insights, and additional concepts that you would like to explore on your own.

We have covered a lot of spiritual territory together, from Divine love, to respecting the Earth, building a community, and the nature of the cosmos! This exploration was meant to introduce you to a variety of thoughts, ideas, and topics that you can investigate further if you choose. I have also led you through a typical daily spiritual practice that I use myself: morning readings, prayers, and activities; followed by time for reflection in the evening.

Feel free to follow this example as you go forward, substituting in your own readings and prayers. I have a few books that might make good morning reading listed in the "Additional Resources" section starting on page 246, or feel free to use your own devotional or inspirational texts as well. Alternatively, you can branch out from here and create an entirely different spiritual practice for yourself. The choice is always yours.

At the very least, I hope that you come away from this program with an understanding of the importance of devoting short amounts of time to yourself and Spirit on a daily basis. Regular time and attention can enhance your connection to the Divine, bring more awareness to your life, enhance intuition and creativity, and give you more of a sense of calm in this sometimes chaotic world.

I want you to remember this as we part ways: You are a gift. You are a miracle. A rare treasure. A beautiful expression of divinity, now and always.

My prayer for you: I send you heartfelt love and gratitude for taking this journey with me. May your days be blessed and filled with love, joy, and meaning beyond your wildest imaginings!

3 Celebrate Your Wins

On the following pages, keep track of the successes you have during the time you work on this journal. Also write down good things that happen to you, compliments you receive, or good things people say about you. Alternately, start a separate "Celebrations" journal so that you can track your successes in one place. Go back and review these wins when you need a bit of an emotional boost.

Date	Positive Event / Success / Win

Date	Positive Event / Success / Win

Date | Positive Event / Success / Win

Date	Positive Event / Success / Win

Date _____ Positive Event / Success / Win _____

4 Additional Practices

Use the practices below to add to your experience of this program, or substitute one of these for a practice that is suggested in the daily readings.

Be An Angel to Others

Goal: Spread love, compassion, and kindness to others.

A practice that may simply evolve on its own as you continue on your path is learning how to be an "angel" for someone else. At its most basic, it means respectfully giving your time, knowledge, experience, kindness, or affluence to assist someone else who needs it.

Many religions and philosophies have a very interesting view of the spiritual beings that we call angels. We may think of them as Divine messengers, or even souls who help further the cause of truth and light. But too many of us seem to wait around hoping that these otherworldly beings will somehow miraculously intervene on this planet and make everything suddenly better, for the good of everyone.

Maybe they will someday.

But what if I told you that *you* can be the pathway that Spirit uses to bring love and light to this world? Through your actions of love and kindness, you can be a messenger of the Divine to this planet, right here and now. You can act in place of the angels. How?

Be an angel for someone else.

Being an angel could be as simple as a recurring monetary donation to a charity you feel is doing Divine work on this planet, or extending kindness from the heart, especially when someone is in a crisis, angry, upset, or grieving.

Other ideas include:

1. Listen deeply: Listen intentionally, without formulating what *you* want to say in return.
2. Pay it forward: Pay a stranger's bill at the coffee shop, toll booth, restaurant, the grocery store, or whatever you can afford.
3. Volunteer your time to assist in a cause that you believe is furthering Divine love on this planet.
4. Assist according to your means: help out at a food bank, volunteer at a homeless shelter, deliver meals to the elderly, or mentor a teen in scholastic or business success.
5. Be an angel to animals, nature, and the Earth: foster rescued pets, work for conservation organizations, garden organically, etc.
6. Buy your local first responders gift cards to a local coffee shop or restaurant.
7. Volunteer to read to folks at a nursing home or hospice.
8. Put money on a stranger's layaway bill.
9. Donate coloring books and crayons to a local children's hospital.
10. Sign up to be a bone marrow or organ donor.
11. Tip generously.
12. Leave flowers or a card for someone who has had a bad day. Is someone in your office or neighborhood going through a rough time? Buy her or him a little

bouquet of cut flowers and leave it on her desk, anonymously. A small, friendly bouquet that you leave one time is enough to tell your coworker or neighbor that someone cares.
13. Put a "Have a Wonderful Day" note in a library book, on a seat on the bus, or at a table in your workplace's cafeteria. I'll admit that this wasn't my idea. I was recently the recipient of a note like this in a book from my local library. It made me smile! Don't write on the book itself, simply write the note on a separate piece of paper and slip it into the middle of the book.
14. Be an angel to your family:
    - Dedicate electronics-free time to spend with your loved ones. Focus on being truly present with each other, not with screens.
    - Hide a fun or romantic note for your spouse or partner to be found later, just because.
    - Teach your children how to prepare healthy food for themselves.
    - Learn and practice healthy, conscious communication with your partner. Soulful, honest communication builds love and trust.
    - Listen to your kids carefully, and without interrupting. Giving them your full attention shows them how important they are to you.

Be Kind to Yourself

Goal: Learn to give yourself love and kindness.

Here are a few ways to be kind to yourself:

1. Go for a walk with a good friend.
2. Eat a healthy breakfast (no sugar, please).
3. Dedicate time to a favorite hobby.
4. Sit in the morning sunshine with a warm mug of coffee or tea and just *be*.
5. Spend time with your friends: the two-legged or four-legged kind.
6. Smell the roses (buy yourself some flowers), then take the time to really enjoy them.
7. Watch a favorite comedy movie.
8. Make more time for sleep, or a nap.
9. Put on your favorite music and dance.
10. Re-read your favorite book.
11. Review all of the good stuff that has happened to you (see the "Celebrate Your Wins" section of this book).
12. Have a real, deep, meaningful conversation with friends about how you are feeling and what is going on in your life.
13. Pause and enjoy the sunrise (or sunset).
14. Laugh more.

The God Jar

Goal: Ask for guidance without attachment to an outcome.

Get a large, attractive jar or vase, and make sure it is clean. Choose one that has special meaning if you'd like. Bless it with a prayer such as, "God/Spirit/Divine, I know that I don't need to do everything myself so I humbly ask for your help. Thank you for helping me by taking on the concerns I give to you in this jar." This is now your God jar.

Next, prepare several small pieces of paper, each a few inches square, and keep them in a handy location near your God jar. When you have a worry, a situation that seems out of your control, or would like help from Spirit about a challenge in your life, write about it on one of those little slips of paper. Now fold up the paper, put it in the God jar, and thank Spirit for handling this issue for you. As you place your slip of paper in the God jar, go into your heart-space and make an intention to let Spirit handle it for you, for your best and highest good. You can even say something like, "Spirit, I'm stuck and am requesting your help on this challenge I hold in my hands. Please handle this for me in a way that is for my best and highest good."

Place your request in the God jar, then forget about it.

Next is the most important part: continue on with your day. Whatever challenge or question you had is now on Spirit's to-do list, not yours. Spirit is working on taking care of the issue for your highest good, and you can rest because it's now out of your hands.

When I use the God jar, I find that it's best if I completely forget about the issues that I place inside and stay unattached to a particular outcome. Then I try to patiently and calmly wait for a sign that Spirit has intervened.

You may receive the clarity you need from an unexpected source, or you might see the situation resolve quickly, seemingly by itself. When it happens, take a moment to thank Spirit for stepping in to help you.

Love Meditation

Goal: A deeper connection to the Divine, and sharing love with the world.

Do this meditation any time you want to strengthen the field of love around you:

1. Sit in a quiet place with no distractions, and where you can safely keep your eyes closed.
2. Take three deep breaths to calm and settle yourself, then breathe normally.
3. On each inhale, visualize Divine love-energy coming in to your body.
4. On each exhale, visualize yourself sending waves of love-energy out from your heart.
5. Make those waves of love any color that feels right to you.
6. Let these waves of love drift out into your home, your neighborhood, or town; don't try to control them, just let them flow to where they are needed.
7. Do this for up to five minutes if you're new to it, working up to 10 minutes three times per week

Love Walks

Goal: Resetting your view of the world and training your brain to see the good.

Start out on a 10-15 minute walk (or more, if you're comfortable). As you walk, simply observe your surroundings and look for any evidence of love around you. This could be a mother holding a baby, kids having fun playing together in the park, maybe a dog rolling with reckless abandon in a pile of leaves, or an elderly couple devoted to each other and taking a slow walk together. Whenever you see any evidence of love, pause for a moment. Appreciate having witnessed it, try to feel deeply grateful, and say a little "thank you" for having seen or experienced it. I personally go on love walks several times a week.

Mindful Eating[8]

Goal: Slow down your eating so that you enjoy and appreciate your food.

Eating mindfully has been shown to reduce the amount of food eaten and contributes to weight loss. Practicing mindful eating can help with weight management, control bingeing, and prevent emotional eating.

Start easy: When you eat, use a smaller plate size. A salad or dessert-sized plate is good (six to eight inches across). In the USA, we have gotten used to eating from huge plates ten to twelve inches across, and this gives us a false visual cue of what constitutes a proper serving size. Our brains usually want us to fill the plate, which causes us to overeat. When we give ourselves a smaller plate, we also tend to dish out and consume less food.

For the next three weeks whenever you eat, serve your food on a small plate, sit down at a table, and take a few moments to feel and express gratitude for your food. Then as you eat, focus on the food you are eating. Refrain from talking with others, or at minimum only engage in pleasant conversation. No arguments. No reading. No media (computers, mobile devices, internet, television, etc.). Eat slowly. Relax. Focus on your food. Savor it as you chew. Stop eating when you feel satisfied.

The next level: Take time between bites. Put down your utensil for a few moments. Again, savor the flavor of the food or drink as you consume it. Chew well. Avoid rushing.

Alternatively, try eating with your non-dominant hand. This will force you to slow down and allow feelings of satiety to reach your brain before you overeat.

Sacred Word Contemplation

Goal: A quieter mind.

Sacred word contemplation is a great way to both quiet your mind and embrace yourself with positive, spiritual energy.

---

[8] If you have an eating disorder, please check with your health care provider before doing this exercise.

1. Sit and quiet your mind while relaxing your muscles.
2. Close your eyes and breathe normally.
3. Choose a sacred and positive word to work with during this session.
4. Example: love, God/Spirit/Creator, Buddha, Jesus, peace, joy, freedom, etc.
5. Repeat that one word silently to yourself for at least 10 minutes.
6. Allow yourself to become one with that word. If you lose focus, that's OK. Just refocus on your sacred word.
7. Start with 10-minute sessions, working up to 20-minute sessions over time.

Silent Prayer

Goal: A deeper connection to the Divine.

People can be pretty talkative. We speak out loud to communicate our thoughts and feelings to one another. Most of us have an inner voice, too: our ego perhaps, or our fears, or we may even mimic what we heard long ago from a parent or spouse. Some of us talk in our sleep, and often we talk when we pray or meditate.

I am not saying that talking is a bad thing. But I want to offer a suggestion that perhaps it might be fun to mix it up a little and try a less vocal way to pray.

During my near-death experience (NDE), my spiritual Guide mentioned a practice that I did not understand right away. She told me that while the Divine loves all of our prayers, we might consider sometimes praying in silence. She told me that silencing with the voice and mind, both, was another way to connect with Spirit. She also said that she did not necessarily mean meditation. It was a form of prayer to which she referred.

It took me a year before I thought deeply about that particular lesson. When I did, I assumed that she meant either sacred word contemplation (which I do daily), or engaging in favorite activities in which our ego minds could go silent (hiking, running, gardening, knitting, etc.). While these can bring great benefits to us, in hindsight I think she was talking about something else. It's truly a form of silent, devotional, loving prayer and appreciation.

Here is one way to practice silent prayer:

1. Spend some quiet time filling your heart, mind, and physical body with a positive feeling-state such as love. How? Think about someone you love deeply and allow that love-feeling to fill your body, mind, and soul.
2. Let go of the need to have words in your mind while you do this. Words are not necessary. Focus instead on the positive *feeling-state* of love. It's OK if words are in your mind at first but with practice, I'll bet you'll find that the positive feeling becomes so strong that it overcomes any desire for words.
3. Let go of the need to *do* something, too. Just *be*.
4. Try to bask in that positive, high-vibrational feeling-state for a few moments. Let it wash over you and through you. Focus on the feeling of love, and send it to Spirit.
5. Allow yourself to *be* this feeling of love for as long as you can.

Tithe

Goal: Help others and yourself by keeping the energy of love flowing.

Do you give back to those around you? Do you perform works in service or support organizations that help others?

How do you give back? And more importantly, why bother?

Charitable giving or tithing is a practice that I resisted for a long time. I know a lot of folks do not see the value in it, and some don't feel that they have enough money to spare. But I've found out just how important *giving* is to keep the energy of love flowing in the world around me.

Modern tithing is understood to be a gift of 10% of what you receive, given to a person or organization you feel is doing Divine work on this planet. If you cannot afford 10%, start by giving what you can. If you cannot afford to tithe money right now, consider giving of your time and expertise instead.

During my NDE, I learned some important lessons about the concepts of giving. Giving back to others, *in whatever way we can afford it*, helps us keep our hearts open and connected to God. It can also help us strengthen our bonds to our fellow humans and shore up the structures of our communities. Done with a freely open heart, giving back is a way that we can express love, compassion, and kindness to each other, our world, and to Spirit. And one other thing you might have noticed: giving just simply *feels good*. I sometimes wonder if the good feelings that come from freely giving to others is Spirit's little built-in reward for being of service.

Your Miraculous Life and World

Goal: Build a vision of your best, most expansive life, and create a vision for the world.

This is a fun but serious journaling exercise, so grab a pen and your notebook (or your computer) and dive in. You may also want to create art or music to accompany your vision of a miraculous future.

Give yourself at least an hour to envision and write about this:

If you had no fears, and all of your needs were taken care of, what would your life look like? How would it be different from your current life, and what would be the same? What would you do every day? Where would you live? Who would be with you? Would you volunteer your time to help a cause? If so, which one(s)? Make sure to describe your health, your relationships, your spirituality, how you spend your time, your finances, and any hobbies or interests you have.

Once you complete envisioning your miraculous life, write at least another paragraph about the miracle you envision for the world. How would the world function in your personal vision of utopia? What would be different from the way it is now? What problems are solved? Get as detailed as you can.

Some people finish this exercise in an hour, others may spread this out over several days. Take as much time as you need and revise your miracles as often as you like. This exercise is designed to give you a glimpse into your own soul by helping you envision what is truly important to you.

Underline or make notes about the top three to five things that stand out in your personal miracle, and one or two things in your world miracle. For example, you might want to live in Vancouver, Canada, have a spouse and two kids, go sailing at least twice a week, play guitar, and finish your degree in ancient history. For the world, you might envision the end to malnutrition.

Then brainstorm ways you can take steps to start making some of these things a reality. For example, if your dream life involves playing guitar, can you start taking lessons now?

One optional add-on to this exercise is to read your complete miracle to yourself every day. I usually do this in the morning just after I finish eating my breakfast. It gives me a positive start to the rest of the day.

5 Additional Resources

Below are additional resources that might help you as you continue on your spiritual journey:

Amen, Dr. Daniel: *Change Your Brain, Change Your Life*

Axe, Dr. Josh: *Eat Dirt*

Callanan, Maggie R.N.: *Final Gifts*

Collette, Amy: *The Gratitude Connection*

Dossey, Larry: *One Mind*

Dyer, Dr. Wayne: *The Power of Intention*

Earle, Dr. Sylvia: *Sea Change: A Message of the Oceans*

Falco, Howard: *I Am*

Frankl, Dr. Viktor: *Man's Search for Meaning*

Fuhrman, Dr. Joel: *Eat for Life*

Greene, Dr. Brian (books and video): *The Fabric of the Cosmos; The Elegant Universe; The Hidden Reality*

Janssen, Jeff: *10 Life-Changing Lessons from Heaven*

Laszlo, Ervin: *The Akashic Experience*

Moriarty, Christine: *Creating Your Moneypeace*

Parnia, Dr. Sam: *Erasing Death* and *What Happens When We Die?*

Robinson, Lynn: *Divine Intuition*

Ruiz, don Miguel: *The Four Agreements*

Rynes, Nancy: *Awakenings from the Light*

Radin, Dr. Dean: *Entangled Minds* and *Real Magic*

Taylor, Dr. Travis: *The Science Behind the Secret*

About Nancy Rynes

Nancy Rynes is an inspirational speaker, artist, and author of ***Awakenings from the Light*** and ***Messages from Heaven***, both books detailing the lessons she learned from two near-death experiences (NDEs). She is a spiritual explorer, making the path to a peace-filled life clearer for seekers all over the world. Nancy is also a leading voice for bringing eternal, spiritual wisdom into our lives on Earth, developing our heart-centered intuition, and living a life of inspired creativity. Known for her fun, lighthearted, girl-next-door demeanor, Nancy loves teaching others how to live a more purposeful, joyful, creative, and spiritually-inspired life.

For more information on Nancy and her current classes, workshops, and events, see:

NancyRynes.com

Her artwork is available at:

NancyRynesStudio.com

Credits

Photos (Creative Commons Licenses)
Anncapictures; Conger Design; Elmer Geissler; FoYu; Free-Photos; Gab-Rysia; Gerd Altmann; InspiredImages; NmewahanG; PICNIC-Foto-Soest; Pixource; Sasin Tipchai

Graphics (Creative Commons Licenses)
Clker-Free-Vector-Images; Gordon Johnson; Mohammed Hassan; Nora_29; OpenClipart-Vectors; truthseeker08; Xiao feng Lew

Cover Photo
Serhii Yurkiv, courtesy Shutterstock

Cover and Interior Designs
Nancy Rynes

Author Photo
L. Guy McWethy

Printed in Great Britain
by Amazon